TALES OUT OF SCHOOL

Jeannette Ellwood

First published in Great Britain in 2016 by Sanyeh Publishing

Sanyeh Publishing
e-mail marion.ellwood@hotmail.co.uk

My gratitude goes to Tim Atkinson who pointed me in the right direction and continues to give support and advice.

Special thanks go to Stephanie Dickens for her many words of wisdom and best cups of tea ever.

I would never have got this far without the special skills of Martine Cherry who gave up her precious time in her busiest of schedules.

Derek Prescott our superb local photographer dropped everything to get the cover into working order, many thanks.

Inky Mitch – Ian Mitchell designed a fun front cover to catch the eye of my readers...thank you for your artistry.

Last of all hugs and thanks to Peter Ellwood my husband, ever patient...

Author's Note

I first read Flora Thompsons's 'Larkrise to Candleford' in my early twenties. I was entranced by the portraits she painted of the real life and times in those Oxfordshire villages so long ago.

I loved the descriptions of the countryside, unspoilt and verdant. I loved the intertwining tales of the villagers and marvelled at the wealth of experiences she shared with us. I never expected to live in a Hertfordshire village that echoed the character and events she described so vividly – but by chance I did.

My Tales are a memory-mix of real people and real happenings in a real setting. They all sprang into glorious colour as I relived and wrote about those episodes of my former life.

I hope I will be forgiven any dramatic enhancements or errors of memory I have made in the retelling. They are entirely my fault. Put them down to the imperfect recollections of a now doddery ex village schoolteacher.

There is no doubt to my mind the people of that beautiful Chiltern Village were very special, I will remember all of them, always.

Jeannette Ellwood (formerly Armer)
Carrick Castle,
Cairndow.

January 2016

List of Chapters

Introduction

'What we want to see is the child in pursuit of knowledge and not knowledge in pursuit of the child.'

George Bernard Shaw

I fell into the job almost by accident.
I had very recently qualified as a teacher at time when there was a shortage of primary school teachers. I did the fast track course as a mature student, came out with an English Hons. qualification – not very useful – and a teaching certificate, which got me an instant job.

My 'interview' was casual in the extreme. I heard through the village grapevine the Reception class teacher had just left the village school and they needed a replacement, so I rang Mr W, the Head of the Village School.

'Come for a cup of tea this afternoon, about four. I will give you a tour of the school' he said.

The large Victorian School building, a stone's throw from the graveyard and the church, was at the end of a blooming, heaven-scented, privet hedge lined drive. The heavy studded front door, with its key still in the lock, was open to let in the late summer sunlight.
Mr W., a shortish, pleasant looking man sporting a red bow tie, welcomed me on the doorstep.

'Hullo, you must be Mrs A. do you like water colours?' He greeted me with a smile, and led me straight into his office where he had several paintings arranged on the floor leaning against his chair, desk and wall.

'They are delightful,' I said enthusiastically. 'I especially like this one.' it was a soft sunset view of the Chiltern Hills.

'Yes,' he said 'that was done last year. I think it is the best...' He trailed off obviously thinking deeply.

'Here.' He announced. 'Here.' and he lifted it and held it against the wall opposite his desk.

'What do you think?'

'Great! Beautiful! You will be able to look at it while you work.' I replied.

'I paint watercolours. I am currently preparing for an Exhibition – in London.' He added, with some pride. He indicated I should sit and drink a cup of tea, resplendently served in beautiful porcelain cups and saucers.
Not the usual teacher-mug-with-a-brew I had become so used to.

'When we have finished I will show you your room.' He sipped his tea slowly, savouring its aroma.
'We are very old fashioned here, but don't worry, I hope to improve the facilities in the near future.' He gazed round his office, looking at each painting in turn.

'Hmm...mmm.' He murmured absently and beckoned me to follow him. As he led me to the Reception classroom, through the hall, all I had time to observe was that the parquet flooring was slightly dusty, and there was a large stove in the corner.

He opened the door to a high ceilinged, brick lined room, painted a very soft off pink, which also housed an extremely black brute of a stove caged behind a wire mesh fire guard with an old fashioned brass rail along the top.

It dominated the scene. The small infant sized tables and chairs shrank to midget proportions in that setting. The teacher's desk was covered with a film of dust and the black oiled floor looked as if it could do with a good sanding down to its original oak splendour. He allowed me an extremely speedy glance round; I was then slightly pushed out of the way as he withdrew, closing the door softly behind us.

'Well that's it.' was all he said.

Back in his office, Mr W got out some papers and pushed them towards me.

'The bureaucrats have to be served, could you fill these in and bring them back with you when you start next week. Our first day of term is Tuesday.'

I was taken aback and asked feebly

'Are you allowed to give me the job - just like that?'

He gave me a beatific smile,

'Oh yes, I don't believe in all these new rules. They hinder progress and cause too much red tape.' He went on 'Would you like an envelope?' He handed me an extremely large one with Dacorum Education Office, already printed on the front.

'You can deal with all the formalities,' he instructed me. 'Make sure your references are in order and enclose details of your qualifications, I am sure we will work very well together.' He held out his hand, and stood up.

'You have fifteen children in the class, some very naughty boys and one or two really nice little girls. I am sure they will enjoy you as a teacher. I want everyone to be happy.'

We shook hands and he closed that formidable front door behind me. I heard the key turn in the lock.

He was very eager to get back to his paintings.

As I walked home clutching the Education Office's envelope, I looked at the beauty of the surrounding hills. I could smell the hedgerow's aromatic perfume mix of hawthorn, *rosa canina* and blackthorn.

I got a smile from a couple of women I met walking along Newground Road, towards the house I had recently moved into and I enjoyed the view of fields and trees as I walked. It was an alluring scenario.

However, in spite of my love of the countryside, and the friendliness of the people, I thought:

'I am mad to even consider a job in an old fashioned dirty school, with an absent-minded eccentric Head and 'naughty' boys, whatever the word 'naughty' means.

I would be wise to accept that job in the Primary School with the up-to-the minute Headmistress and spotless classroom, with all the modern equipment.'

My tutor at University - and others - had already warned me that whilst teaching in a village school environment offered unique opportunities, it required a certain sort of person to cope with its idiosyncrasies.

'Aim for a good urban school they had advised. Take a further qualification and apply for headships when you have gained a little experience. A stint in a village school will *not* enhance your career prospects. Don't forget, it takes a certain sort of person to sink into country life.'

I looked at the envelope in my hand, I remembered the eccentric, amiable Head and thought of the children whose ancestors had lived in the village for generations, who made their mark there, who had died there, perhaps I too could become part of that living history.

I remembered the local paper saying that newcomers were changing the face of the countryside; maybe I could also help change the face of village education?

It would be a challenge. I loved challenges.

It would mean me taking a chance with my new career. Taking a chance? Hurray!

I felt a stirring of interest; I would hate to miss a possible adventure…possibly even a life changing experience.

I took a deep breath and I jumped in with both feet forgetting my earlier aims of achieving a headship.

I would embrace village life, deep in the beauty of Ashridge Forest and the surrounding Chiltern Hills, and relish the peculiarities of the present Head of that relic of Victoriana - the delightful rural school. Which is why I spent the next fifteen years or so living and working in the rich and heady mix of interesting, sometimes eccentric local people, leavened by newcomers, and teaching children who crept under my skin, into my life and remain in my memory forever.

This unique kaleidoscope of experience certainly broadened my outlook. It introduced me to people I would never have met in the anonymity of a town and gave me an all too brief glimpse into a way of life that was passing before my eyes.

I never found out whether I was that 'certain sort of person', my tutor had described to me, all I can say is that I wouldn't have missed those halcyon village school days, with its mixture of pain and tears, pleasure and laughter, for anything.

A Touch of Class

'Phone for the fish knives, Norman
As cook is a little unnerved;
You kiddies have crumpled the serviettes
And I must have things daintily served.

Are the requisites all in the toilet?
The frills round the cutlets can wait
Till the girl has replenished the cruets...'

John Betjeman – How to get on in Society

My first encounter with people from Aldbury happened while I was getting ready for my new term at the primary School. We had not long moved to The Lodge, our house on the edge of the village, and I spent some time wondering about the sort of people we would meet, what they would be like and how we would fit in. I was in for a big surprise. Our first meeting with the neighbours turned out to be a Close Encounter of a Very Special Kind!

The Craufurd family lived in a Victorian-museum sort of house, situated on the edge of Ashridge Forest, not far from The Lodge. Sir James, Lady Ruth's husband was a retired barrister. He was the third son of Alice Wood, daughter of R.M. Wood, who had been a Rector of Aldbury sometime in the twenties. A portrait of that formidable old gentleman was in the Memorial Hall, next to the Shop, in the centre of the village.

Sir James was notorious for his dangerous habit of walking in a leisurely fashion down the centre of the road, his silver-topped cane in one hand, and his occasional doffing of the panama hat resting on his head with the other, ignoring any traffic that wanted to pass. He would possessively gaze from left to right at the pretty cottages and well-kept gardens as he walked slowly along. Only strangers and incomers tooted their horns. Villager-owned cars patiently followed behind knowing he was going to turn off at the pond to go to the shop for The Times, his daily paper.

He ignored them all anyway, maintaining an unvaried pace, whatever traffic snarls took place at his rear. Everyone accepted his assured position as leader of the local community; no one ever questioned his actions and certainly not his authority.

That particular morning I was really busy, cleaning out a store next to the kitchen that had been used to house coal and which still had a thick layer of black dust and whole regiments of spiders... I stopped reluctantly to answer a somewhat peremptory knock at the front door, very aware I was not looking my best.

A tall, thin lady stood in front of me dressed in a misshapen tweed skirt, a somewhat grubby twinset and pearls and an old hat stuck on the top of greying hair. She wore thick stockings, 'sensible' shoes and carried a small jar of honey in her hand. She looked me up and down.

'May I speak with your mistress?
Is she in?' She demanded. She continued after a slight pause and a closer look,
'You are the maid I presume?'
My jaw dropped slightly.
'It's me, er, I am the mistress, and er... I am in.' it took a moment or two for me to stammer.
'We are Sir James and Lady Ruth Craufurd and we live at Brightwood.
My husband is father to the village.' She said by way of introduction. 'I work for the good of the Church. I do hope you attend the services, my good woman.' She carried on, 'Perhaps you sing? My daughter in law, Catherine, takes the choir. She is an Opera singer you know.'
At that point she produced a small green booklet from the old-fashioned wicker basket she had placed at her feet. 'You must have one of these...'

As I started to thank her, she continued 'It costs £1.10s, and here is some honey.' She handed me the jar, 'That will be 2/6d.'

As I turned to put them on the chair in my tiny hall, she came in past me and went directly into my chaotic kitchen that still had breakfast things on the table. Casting an eagle eye round as she went, she peered out of my back door, looked in the old coal store and returned without a word through my sitting room and back to the hall where I remained, transfixed with surprise.

'I know of a cleaning woman in the village, I will tell her to come and see you, you certainly need a good maid.'
She held out her hand; somehow I automatically gave her mine, so we shook hands.

'We are having a few people for drinks…' she paused, obviously wondering if what she was about to say was entirely appropriate, in my lowly social circumstances '…and what does your husband do?'

'He works for the Department of Scientific and Industrial Research, he is a research scientist.' I replied.

'Oh… unexceptional, quite unexceptional.' She murmured looking at me obviously somewhat relieved. 'And you?'

'I'm a school teacher.'

'Oh, well, yes, so that's all right I suppose. Very good.' She took a breath. 'Yes, do come for sherry, next Thursday, 6 o'clock - sharp'
She turned to go. 'You may pay me then, £1.12/6d. Please don't forget.'

As she picked up her basket, which had remained on my step, she looked at my long reddish hair and said, 'Quite nice, mine was as long as yours you know, Sir James, my husband used to admire it. Of course that was a year or so ago.' With that, she abruptly turned away and strode up the drive turning left at the gate, back towards the village. I closed the front door, collapsed onto the bottom two stairs feeling thoroughly unnerved, but then started to laugh. I as sure she had almost been about to ask me to help in her house, as her maid!
What was it she had said?
Had she really called her husband, "father" to the village, *Father* to the village? How had he managed that, I wondered hazily, had he exercised droit de seigneur, when the Lord of the Manor had his way with all young brides?
My thoughts were chaotic, surely not, not even in the depths of rural England...
No not possible. Of course not.
Anyway, he must be well into his seventies. I looked at the booklet I had paid so much for, 'Country Women at War' it said 'Ruth, Lady Craufurd.'

Returning to my cleaning job in the coal hole, I thought about the encounter and my heart sank. What if a Craufurd child was in my class, or indeed what if there were lots of families like that in my new school? How on earth would I cope with the parents let alone the children…?

I already knew that Lady Ruth and her husband were formidable figures in the eyes of many people in the village. Quite a few of the families lived in Craufurd property, and so were dependent on their goodwill. I suppose to do her justice she hid a kind heart, although that was too often hidden behind her brusque manner of speaking.

She made judgements and decisions for the villagers whenever she saw fit. She felt she had a right, indeed a duty, to arrange all village matters - irrespective of village wishes. However, in spite of her benevolent intentions, local people were beginning to find her attitude hard to swallow, alien as it was to this modern age. The Craufurd's role of 'Squire and Lady' was becoming redundant, benevolent dictatorship was definitely going out of fashion.

Her autocratic way of speaking and assumption of authority also left some of us incomers speechless, unaccustomed as we were to the idea of a rigid social hierarchy ruling our private lives. Most of us had come from towns, so the old village ways were amazingly hard to understand. Integration into a conservative rural scene was going to be quite a challenge for us, I concluded. Would my husband and I eventually fit into a village scheme of things, being neither villagers nor gentry; neither 'fish nor fowl nor good red herring' as my mother would have said – I doubted it.

Oh well, I mused, we must wait and see. We were stuck here now for the next few years, and, actually, weren't challenges one of the reasons I had come here and accepted the job in the first place?

Christmas

'While shepherds washed their socks by night,
All seated round the tub
A bar of sunlight soap came down
And they began to scrub.'

St. Saviour's School, Lewisham, S.E.13 - 1942

I had just settled in to my new job when I rashly agreed to be responsible for the important task of producing the nativity play in our small village school. Each year the children acted some Christmas story in the Victorian hall with its ancient homemade stage complete with curtains hung specially for the occasion.

The Vicar, all the local dignitaries, the Chairman and members of the governing body and most of the parents came to this special event.

A local reporter plus his photographer, both of whom turned up every year, could be seen smoking in the back of the hall.

As a newcomer into the tightly knit village community I was extremely anxious to make a good impression on everyone.

It was the era of child led education, self-expression and the 'integrated day'. Ideally, all aspects of education were child led and managed, with the teacher simply acting as a facilitator. Imbued with fervour and enthusiasm, I was determined I would show them my approach to education was modern progressive, and successful. I set out to impress the audience with my brilliant teaching skills - only to meet with one or two small difficulties.

My first obstacle to exhibiting my talents was 'Mary'.

My class had elected determined, self-willed precocious Jennifer to take the part. There was nothing meek, mild or gentle about her! Her rival for attention and class leadership was Mark, a handsome, studious boy with a stubborn streak. Not your ideal Joseph from Mary's point of view. However, as I pointed out somewhat unsympathetically, when 'Mary' took me aside to protest, 'that's show biz for you darling.' Sorry I can't help with this one.'

A determined group of children from my class duly allocated the lesser parts. I was full of misgivings but I stuck to my guns - and my ideology- of a 'child led and managed' production and started rehearsals.

Our first scene was the Angel Gabriel visiting Mary. She was supposed to be meekly sitting at home waiting for the Message from 'on High'. Unfortunately, that was not her style.

'I want to wear my party dress' announced Mary to all and sundry 'it's pink with a standing-out skirt and spangles all over it. My mummy made it for me.'

'...Erm, that isn't really what Mary would be wearing – remember some of the pictures I showed you?' I remonstrated gently.

'I don't care,' came the reply 'I am going to wear my ballet shoes too!' (Jennifer was an aficionado of the ballet as her mother was a dance teacher.) I smiled sweetly, falsely, and mentally shrugged my shoulders.

'All right, Jennifer, if that really is your view of Mary's dress sense, I suppose that's your decision.' She gave me a darkling look as she made for the dressing room.

The children had set the stage, putting Wendy House chairs from our class round a table complete with an electric kettle minus its plug, and assorted mugs. Our classroom's potted palm, placed stage left, was doing duty as an olive tree, reminding Gabriel where he was to make his entrance.

We had rehearsed various lines of script over the previous few weeks. Admittedly it had changed with each rehearsal as the children merrily ad libbed as the mood took them, but everyone seemed to know what they were going to say so the reasonably accurate bare bones of the story emerged as we went on.

Apparently, unknown to me, Mary had decided to do some housework while waiting for the Angel Gabriel, and turned up on the night with a bright yellow duster and a dustpan and broom, ready in the wings, raring to go on.

I on the other hand was extremely nervous as I peeped alternately between the curtains to look at the audience and then through the door to the room where the actors were corralled, waiting to make their entrances.

As per tradition, the hall was full. To my horror the local Education Officer, who was renowned for her sarcastic remarks about anything she took exception to, could be seen sitting beside the Chair of Governors.

Jennifer's mother, grandmother and father were sitting in the front row with Mark's parents and older brother immediately behind them. Everyone looked expectant, anticipating an evening to remember.

The school band run by our head teacher started the first carol. Everyone studied his or her carol sheets and more or less started singing.

The curtains opened and Mary pirouetted onto the stage and stood poised for dramatic effect.

The singing died away as the audience took in her full glory. Tutu quivering, duster waving and dustpan in hand Mary commanded total attention. She smiled sweetly and turned to the nearest chair giving it a hearty rub with her duster.

'I'm doing the housework' she announced 'I know Mary's mummy would like a nice clean house for when visitors come' As she picked up the kettle she moved to front of stage and addressed her mother in the front row,

'This hasn't got HOT water in it because my Teacher wouldn't let me plug it in, Joseph will have to have COLD tea. It's not FAIR, he should have hot tea, cold tea is horrible' and she waved it about dramatically then almost slammed it back onto the somewhat rickety table which shivered in protest... She proceeded to dust the mugs, taking out a teabag she had hidden down the front of her tutu. She put it into her favourite mug, with the cat motif.

'He's late again' she said, arms akimbo, as we heard a tentative off-stage knock.

A figure appeared in what looked like a Dunelm dressing gown with wings from the local Accessorise shop sticking out at the back.

'I didn't say 'Come in!' Anyway you aren't near the tree - go out and come in again.' hissed Mary

Gabriel looked sheepish, blushed and meekly turned back and re-emerged just behind the 'olive' tree stage left. He stood on one leg for some reason and spoke:

'I've got some good news for you,' long pause '...er tiddings 'he looked at the crumpled bit of paper he had clutched in his hand. 'No... tie-d –ings of big happiness and...' He stopped abruptly.

'Great joy' came a voice from the back of the hall (his brother?) Mary turned to the audience and said indignantly,

'This is OUR Play, if you keep shouting like that you will PUT US OFF!'

The brother looked suitably abashed.

'Yes?' she looked kindly at Gabriel, 'what else have you got to tell me?'

'You're pregnant – it's a boy –you will call him Jesus.' stammered Gabriel.

Mary's kindly look disappeared in a flash

'I TOLD you I don't like that name, remember I said Darren, I am not having 'Jesus,' I like DARREN.'

She repeated it very loudly looking first at the hapless angel and then at the audience.

'DARREN!' she almost shouted.

By this time, audience attention was breathlessly captured. Utter silence prevailed.

The reporter from the local paper looked slightly stunned but the hall flashed like a disco with the photographer taking photos first of the stage then of various members of the audience – focussing I regret to say on the expression on the Education Officer's face. For the first time the angel looked determined

'You can't change his name. It's God's baby and what He says goes. Always.' He asserted. 'Anyway Teacher said it was already written in the Book, you know – that special Book, The Bible. It says the baby's name was 'Jesus'.'

I had some hopes he was remembering us all talking about God's omnipotence and omniscience. Maybe some of my words in RE had lodged somewhere.

He delivered his exit line,

'Remember, it's not Joseph's son, it's not even just your son, it's God's and he is jolly pleased with you for being so helpful.

Goodbye, goodbye.' He waved cheerfully at the audience and almost skipped off the stage obviously thrilled his bit was over. Mary muttered some words under her breath, which thankfully no one heard, and turned back to the table to pick up the kettle when Joseph unexpectedly appeared stage right.

He was resplendent in a striped kaftan with a Homebase stripey tea-towel on his head.

Mary eyed him with disfavour.

'What are you doing here it's too soon, I'm making tea and you're supposed to be carpentering until I've finished except

that Miss has taken away the plug so I can't have hot water, only cold.' Resentfully she delivered her lines without pausing for breath.

'I know that' said Joseph, nose in air 'I can't wait all day I've got customers to see to. I don't want tea anyway.'

Mary's colour rose 'You can't change it all now, we agreed what to do. You've GOT to have tea. If you don't you're horrible. You'll spoil it. You're too stuck up anyway, a-a-and now - I really don't like you.'

'I'm your feeancee, I don't want no tea,' asserted Joseph, 'you have to like me, and you have to do what I tells you, it sez so in the Bible.'

His carefully cultivated received English faded in the stress of the moment.

Mary dropped the duster she had been holding all this time and advanced, threateningly, arms akimbo, towards Joseph, who to give him credit, stood his ground.

'Oh no I don't, I'm not even married to you, and I wouldn't marry you anyway. You're bossy. Bossy boots, bossy boots.' She chanted.

'You've got summat to tell me' he said, stemming the flow, 'Remember the angel came to h'announce summat.'

Mary looked triumphant

'Oh yes, he came. He's much nicer than you I'm going to marry him when I am 14.' She paused to see what effect that had on Joseph.

He remained scornfully unimpressed.

'Anyway,' she said 'I'm in the club, and it's a boy, and I'm going to call it Darren NOT Jesus - AND what's more, it's not even yours.'

With that, she flounced off, stage-left, kicking the dustpan out of her way as she went.

There was a stunned silence.

The two children in charge of closing the curtains valiantly pulled on the ropes but they stuck half way giving the audience ample time to see Joseph walking quickly to the table and extract the two chocolate biscuits Mary had hidden in one of the larger mugs in case of imminent starvation during her act.

The clapping started slowly and grew in momentum as the impact of Mary's last words sunk in.

The Nativity scene came next with lots of four and five year olds being either sheep or cherubs. Jennifer, deciding to be producer, had organised it entirely to her satisfaction...

The Angels sang the shepherds did their bit; the Kings turned up on time, although there was one tense moment when Mary said her mum used Boots baby cream not myrrh for her baby, and why hadn't they brought Boots cream?

The newly arrived king, with his dangerously precarious crown, looked affronted at having his present sent back, but after a few heated words, the myrrh was allowed to join 'frank's scents' and the gold, under the crib with real hay in it.

As the last carol echoed round the high ceiling of our lofty Victorian hall, the audience clapped and stamped (brothers again?) their appreciation. The head came and gave me a tight reassuring hug as he wended his way hastily to the actors' noise ridden corral, and I died a thousand deaths hidden just behind the curtain.

I was waiting for Damocles, in the form of the Chair of Governors, to drop his sword resoundingly on my head.

Then amazingly, he stood up and shouted 'Bravo' joining in with the rest of the audience.

Mary's mother was fairly bursting with pride as the reporter rushed to her side for an exclusive interview.

Mary appeared, well in front of the curtain with Gabriel, and did quite a few pirouettes ending with a very creditable curtsey.

The cherubs, lambs, Joseph and baby Jesus clutched in a Shepherd's arms stood well back. Her instructions I presumed. Fortunately, the rag doll that was Jesus, (NOT Darren) didn't seem to object too much.

The photographer rushed up to Mary and asked her to pose with Gabriel...

I was intending to slip away, but too late, the Education Officer asked to see the teacher who had been responsible for the entertainment.

'Well,' she said looking me up and down, 'different...' she lingered over the word. 'Pity about the COLD water though... However, the rest was quite well done.'

At that, Mr Chairman turned to me, gave a wink with his off-side eye, took her arm and escorted her from the hall as she moved with queen like dignity towards the exit pausing only to exchange a few words with the reporter from the local paper. They both turned to look at me, still standing there, rigid. I had a sudden mental vision of what the headlines might be

'Virgin Mary in Tutu calls Jesus 'Darren'.'

Or

'Mary and Joseph Divorced over Angel Wrangle'...

Maybe... something, like that. 'Scary.' I thought. I gulped.

As parents and children found each other voices could be heard 'Did you see me Mum did you, did you...?'and

'You were wonderful darling so very clever...' and the penetrating whisper of one Dad saying thankfully to his wife, 'That's it then I'm off to the Trooper see ya.'

Goodness knows what Mary did after her triumphant photo shoot; probably berate Joseph for taking her chocolate biscuits while she wasn't looking.

As for me I made a run for it - on my bicycle - under cover of the winter dusk, arriving home in time to pour myself a sizeable whiskey, turn on the TV and take the telephone off the hook.

I would wait with bated breath to see the next day's headline, or worse, a visit from the Head requesting my resignation...

'Immediately, please.'

Thankfully only two days until the end of my first term, I breathed a sigh of relief - I couldn't wait.

Cath's AA

'I know you believe you understand what you think I said but I am not sure you realise that what you heard is not what I meant!'

Anon

There was no doubt my classroom was a relic from the past. It was large, lofty, and draughty. The leaded light windows needed re-leading. On windy days they leaked wafts of cold air. The over-oiled floor left black marks on the girls' clean knickers when they sat on it, clustered round me for Story Time. The stove blew dust and occasional clouds of grey-black smoke whenever it felt like it, although the smoke billows did gradually lose themselves in the high beams above our heads. I'd got some rugs for the children to sit on and the fire belched heat on wintry days, so we didn't care; we all loved its glowering presence.

I was so proud of the bright paper panels I lined the Victorian brick-painted walls with, although little would stay for long on the slightly greasy paint. Children's work was dotted at random anywhere I could stick it. My classroom was as ready as I could make it for the start of my new term.

The dominant feature of the whole room was the enormous black 'AA.' I had christened the beast of a stove the 'Ancient Anachronism' the first time I saw it on my tour of the school at my interview. The acronym stuck.

I wondered how it was going to work – I couldn't see me stoking it somehow. I soon learned. The stoves, which graced the classrooms, including the pre-fabricated building out at the back and the school hall, were all tenderly cared for by Cath Barber, the caretaker, cleaner/ handyman.

'Oh boogar 'ere we goes again.' moaned Cath as she tramped in with two buckets of coal so weighty I couldn't even attempt to shift them along the floor let alone carry them.

She was a buxom, muscular woman with a navvy's colourful vocabulary, probably in her mid sixties. She had greyish hair tied back in a sort of bun, and always wore a 'Mrs Mop' type of apron-cum-overall.

Born and bred in the village I don't think she had ever ventured any further than Tring, the nearest town, for the occasional outing.

She viewed me, both teacher and newcomer, with suspicion and distrust.

'Wotz your name, anyway.' She demanded as she walked past me into the classroom. She went on without giving me time to answer.

'I duz everythin' around here...' She leant on her very dirty mop and expounded.

'I comes in at 6 am every mornin', I cleans every classroom, every lavvy and fills them there black beasts with coal every day.

Do I get thanks, no, no-one even sez 'allo, I might as well be the white sprektar. (Does she mean spectre, I thought?)

Mind you, you're the only body 'ere this time o'day. Aint you sceered?'

I looked at her in surprise

'Scared? What of...?'

'Ain't you a-listening?' She interrupted me. 'The sprectre, wot 'aunt's this place. She comes and sceers all the new'uns, reglar. She's white an' she luvs this room special. You'll see 'er sometime, everyone duz. Anyways, Miss wot *are* you doing 'ere this time o'day?' 'Oh... er, I'm not afraid of ghosts, I'm more scared of the County Education officer actually, and she might drop in anytime. I'm a very new teacher,' I continued, 'so I am early because I need to prepare my lessons; also I need time to explore the depths of that cupboard at the end there.'

The said cupboard stretched the whole width of the room and was so deep I would have to crawl into it to reach whatever was hidden if it was right at the back. Rumour had it a previous teacher decided to lock a child in it for punishment and left him there all night, forgotten, confined behind its sturdy doors.

Apparently a very white-faced and trembling lad had been let out by one of the children next morning. The Head teacher of the time had no quarrel with that particular course of action as there was no record of any reprimand or even comment in the logbook.

'That *was* way back in the 'Old Queen's' time.' The old timer had said.

'Presumably Queen Victoria.' I thought. She had died in 1901 so it happened sometime ago, thank goodness.

It was currently a place the play-and-learn equipment was stored, but all I had found that was of use, was a few beads suitable for threading. These were supposedly to help the children develop their motor skills and to learn to count at the same time. I had not yet had time to penetrate its dark, gloomy and damp interior entirely. Maybe it held untold treasures. Who knew?

I wasn't too worried about its contents, I had been given a small budget and had introduced some Cuisenaire rods for maths, the newly popular Ladybird 'Janet and John' reading books, and some games for the playground.

They would do for the moment.

Cath went on with her work. I watched in a fascinated sort of way, as she got out a soot-blackened duster and proceeded to wipe the children's desks and chairs, leaving them somewhat smeary.

She then ran the mop round the edge of the room at a rate of knots leaving a considerable amount of debris in her wake.

Finally, she opened AA, which rewarded her by coughing out a large quantity of soot-laden smoke.

'Boogar, and blarst.' said Cath adding a further couple of expletives not usually heard in school.

I was glad there were no children around.

Making even more soot and fumes, Cath riddled AA with great vigour and poured the entire contents of one bucket into its maw, slamming its door shut at great speed. She straightened up looked at me and placed the other bucket well away from the fire with a slightly malicious look.

'You'll 'ave to fill 'im later.' she announced, picking up mop and duster. With a sideways glance at me, she opened the door and left.

I sat staring at the bucket she had placed at least three feet away from AA.

I experimentally tried to lift it, without success, it must have weight a ton!

I could hear the school bell in the playground, my children skipped into the classroom and my teaching day began.

AA was forgotten.

My morning was bugged with various children coming to me saying   'Please Mrs. A, my clean dress is dirty...' tears would fall and I wrote a note of apology to the parent.

'Please Mrs A. my book is all smudged.' Another child would say and some mite's work would be soot-smeared right across the page.

'Right,' I thought 'time to talk to this Cath.'

Cath had poked her head round the door, at lunchtime to see if the coal bucket had made any progress towards AA. It had not. She grunted, with a satisfied air, looked at me slightly contemptuously (I felt) and disappeared.

By home time AA was decidedly dead...starved of coal he had given up the ghost with a vengeance.

After school, I went to find her. She was in the tool shed, where she usually spent her spare time, drinking tea.

'I've got some chocolate biscuits in my desk,' I seductively murmured. 'Fancy sharing them?'

Two seconds later she arrived, tea in hand, and sat down on *my* chair at *my* desk completely at home there.

I leaned back on the large, solid, brass-topped safety guard in front of AA. There was no heat of course, without Cath's tender ministrations it was stone cold.

'You h'aint given him his lunch!' she grinned evilly 'If you don't feed un midday he dies orlright.'

She took her third Cadburys digestive chocolate biscuit.

'Anyways you should be at 'ome lookin' after 'ubby. Dunnt he mind you working'?'

'Well,' I started to explain, 'We both need to work to pay for the house, and we do have two children. Children are expensive, and I love my horses but they're expensive too.'

'I got kids as well. So I phuck plezants,' she said 'I gets a shillun a go. I got the world record for beein' the fastest plezant phucker in 'ertfordshire.' She took her fourth chocolate digestive, and munched thoughtfully. 'Have you ever...?' she began

'No!' I hastily interrupted, not at all sure what she was going on about.

'I never have.'

Filing what she had said at the back of my mind for later examination, I gently closed the drawer of my desk where the last two biscuits sat.

She got up to go.

'Well, I dun my bit fur today, I'm off got a busy evening, ph...' I stopped her.

'Er, tomorrow, I am on lunchtime playground duty, do you think you could feed AA?' She threw me a shrewd glance.

'I like Garibaldis better'n chocs. I allus hav me tea about four of an arternoon.'

'Right, Garibaldis it is. See you tomorrow.'

'Don't you stay too late here all alone, yon sprektar allus turns up 'bout now. bye bye.'

As I closed the door to go home, in spite of myself, I gave a nervous glance towards that cupboard at the end of the room. If the 'sprektar' was going to appear it would probably be about there.

I thought of the poor little child incarcerated all night. I shivered.

School was suddenly echo filled and gloomy with no one but me in it.

'Sprektars' seemed only too possible in the gloaming of the autumn evening... I quickly walked out locking the front door safely behind me.

The next morning I arrived after Cath had fed AA, mopped the floor and 'cleaned' the children's chairs and work tables.

I noted black smears over the workbooks I had left on my desk. She had obviously used her soot-encrusted duster to remove some of the fine layer of dust that had crept around everything overnight.

I suppose I was honoured. Mr. W, the Head, had told me she wouldn't touch *his* desk!

I put the garibaldi biscuits in my drawer for safekeeping, and set to with my pristine yellow duster from home to make sure all sooty smears were removed from anything either the children or I would be coming in contact with.

My extra 'duties' were to become part of my daily routine.

As the children ran in, Tracy came up to me. She was carrying a black puppy.

'My dog had two.' She said, pushing the little wriggling creature into my hands.

'This one is a girl. She is for you. To keep. Forever.' She was anxious to make it clear it was a present to me from her.

'You do like her don't you?' She looked into my face intently. 'You will keep her?' Her lower lip began to tremble.

The puppy settled into my arms looking round happily at the ring of children's faces surrounding us. They all began to look worried as I wasn't immediately able to think of what to say.

'Please say yes.' Whispered Tracy 'My mum said you was a dog lover, you do love dogs?'

'I can't...' I began. Mrs.C came into the class in a rush.

'I am sorry, Tracy so wanted you to have her she sneaked her in. I didn't realise 'til just now she'd brought her.'

I looked round at the group of eager faces, and looked at Tracy who was beginning to feel her teacher might not measure up to her expectations.

I couldn't do it. I couldn't let them down.

I looked down at the round, fat, tiny cushion-with-a-tail by now curled up on my lap and weakly said,

'Thank you. Of course, I love dogs. I'll take her, when she is ready to leave her mother.'

'That will be at the end of the week. Can you come and get her?' Said Mrs C.

'Yes.' I replied. I looked again at my 'cushion as she lifted her head to gaze trustfully at me, she would fit in well with my Labrador, four cats and five horses I thought with resignation. All my family loved animals she would fit in all right. At such moments history is made. That is how my 'cushion' Twiggy, coupled - literally - with the Vicar's Jack Russell, (together with several others, in the fullness of time!) became the matriarch of the famous 'Aldbury Terriers', and founded a dynasty of very strange looking, but eminently lovable dogs.

Feeling a little bemused, wondering what my long-suffering husband was going to say, I became aware my popularity rating had soared. I was surrounded by beaming faces.

'Right, children time for News...' they rushed, with good will to sort pencils and paper.

'News Time' featured many drawings and short laborious sentences about Mrs. A, and her new puppy, named 'Miss Twiggy' after a mixture of Miss Piggy of Muppet fame and model, Twiggy. The model was extremely thin. Sadly 'Miss Twiggy' wasn't! She took after Miss Piggy in shape and it soon became evident in temperament also.

AA was warm and in a good mood, so there was little smoke, and we were all amazingly clean at the end of the day. Time had passed quickly, as usual; all at once, it was four o'clock.
Cath poked her head round the door, teacup in hand, as I emerged rather breathless from inching my way to the back of the daunting cupboard at the end of my room.
'You kep' the pup then.' She sat herself down in my chair, opening the desk drawer, extracting the garibaldis and closing the drawer with her elbow, all in one practised movement.
'Yes.' I replied rather defensively, I might have guessed she would know everything that went on.
'I knew you was soft, as soon as I set eyes on you,' she remarked. 'wot you found then?'
She looked curiously at the array of things I had in my arms.
There were piles of damp newspapers, various ladies' journals with vintage knitting patterns and recipes together with some craft ideas. They were all disappointing and damply disintegrating.
There were also one or two school logbooks, which had to go to Mr.W. for safekeeping. The entries were written in a copperplate hand and signed Margaret Kitson, a previous head teacher now retired, but still living in the village.
Cath let out a shriek, which made me jump out of my skin.
'That's mine, I did that when I woz the same age as the kiddies in your class. Oh my gawd fancy that still bein' 'ere!' She got up from my chair and moved amazingly quickly down the room to where I was standing.
I looked down at the round, object in my hand.
Its surround was a damaged gilt frame. It had a soft watercolour tinted background and some artificial flowers stuck onto backing paper. Over all was a transparent dome. The whole effect should have been pretty, but it wasn't really, it was too crudely done.
I glanced up at Cath's face. She had tears in her eyes and a tremulous smile on her lips.
'It's a bit of 'istory that's wot it is. I made that sixty years ago. I lorst it. Me mum gave me such a clump when I couldn't find it. She's dead now o' course.'

She suddenly sat down on the nearest chair. 'I woz taken outa the class to work on the fields, we kids did that in them days. We woz allowed to keep the gleanings arter the 'arvest woz in. I 'ad put it on Teacher's desk but it 'ad gorn when I got back the next term.'

My heart melted at the thought of this hard-bitten old lady, mourning the loss of her childish effort at trying to create something beautiful, so very long ago. Impulsively I handed it to her.

'Its yours' I said 'You keep it. I don't know what Mr W. intends to do with these things.'

Actually, I did know, he had instructed me to burn anything that was still in the cupboard. He had partly turned it out when he first came to the school and had, regrettably, at least one bonfire. She looked at me.

'It wouldn't last long in my 'ouse' she said. My boys and my 'ubby isn't keerful.'

She handed the somewhat fragile 'work of art' back to me.

It was hard to believe her large calloused hands had once been small enough to arrange those flowers on the delicate painted background.

'You're a softie,' she said 'you keep it. I bet you got lotsa pikturs at your'ouse.'

I admitted I loved the pictures on my walls. She was right; her art was a bit of history.

'Thank you.' I said 'I will look after it for the School. When the time comes I will give it back, maybe to the village archives, or even a museum.'

I looked at the other object that the cupboard had disgorged. It was about four foot long, very knobbly and had a blackened silver band round it near the top. '**d M**su*' it said. I could just make out those few letters it was all so dirty. It had not seen daylight for many years from the look of it.

'Cath' I called after her, as she returned to her place at my desk. She took another slurp of her tea. 'Would you know what this is?'

I walked over to her holding the stick at arm's length waving it slightly as I went.

She hardly glanced at it.

'Oh yes, that's 'Ole Missus.' She's the one to keep aways from. She 'urt somthin awful. Its them knobs you feel most. The Ole Man used it frequent.'

'You don't mean as a cane do you? Surely Miss Kitson didn't…'

'No, the Ole Man, I says. Wazn't you lissening? E woz 'ead before her. 'E loved Ole' M.

'E kep' her in 'is office so 'e could get at 'er quick. 'E 'ad 'er name put on. It's real silver that is, really real.'

She was obviously impressed with the silver band.

I was horrified at the hard, cruel bumps on it. I tried to imagine what sort of man had children in his care and would like using it so much he gave it a name, a silver label, and kept it handily nearby, in his office. I couldn't. The whole idea was against everything I believed in about teaching and caring for children.

My face showed what I felt, I suppose, because Cath glanced at me again and said,

'Softie.' and ate another garibaldi.

Old Missus was another piece of history I would look after until the time came to put it in its rightful place – perhaps in a local history museum.

I smiled at her,

'We must come to an arrangement about AA, you know. I can't lift those buckets; I would never be able to fill him up enough to keep him going to the end of school time.'

She got up from the chair and looked scornfully at my arms.

'Softies never 'ave good arms, they aint got no strengf, I'd better take care of him.'

She moved to the coal bucket, opened AA's door and effortlessly flung in the whole contents. As she shut his door she muttered to herself,

'That'll keep 'im ot for a while, the boogar.'

As she prepared to leave for home, she turned to pick up a plastic bag that she thrust at me,

'Ive been phucking plezants' she said. 'I brought you a braces. Durnt you worrit about AA, I'll see to 'im. I aint no softie.'

She gave a grim smile, flexed one arm, and closed the door.

As I peered into the plastic bag, light dawned. There, nestling closely together, were two small, naked birds.

Not a feather in sight. She 'phucked plezants' for the men of the local shoot.

The old rhyme jumped into my head...

'I am not the pheasant plucker,
I'm the pheasant plucker's mate
I am only plucking pheasants 'cos the pheasant plucker's running
late'

I tried saying that quickly, and suddenly understood her own pet
phrase for the job that earned her the extra 'shillun's'. Did she have
a sly twinkle in her eye when she first told me about her 'phucked
plezants'?
Was she watching to see my reaction at her choice of words? Was
she testing me for some reason, in her own inimitable way? I'd
probably never find out, but I was very grateful for these two plump
birds that fitted into my Aga oven so nicely, ready to be cooked for
my Sunday lunch.
Thank you 'Good ole Cath!'

****

Cath's 'work of art' is hanging on my bedroom wall biding its time
when it will go into the village archives. It is now just over a
hundred years old.

Another antique reminder of another type of ancient *anachronism*,
not of a blackened old stove, but of a style of education long gone.

Henry

Friends are as companions on a journey, who ought to aid each other to persevere in the road to a happier life.

There is geometry in the humming of the strings, there is music in the spacing of the spheres.

Pythagoras 590-475 BC.

Henry caused a sensation. He addressed Mr. W our head teacher as 'Sir.'
Our village school protocol required pupils to address us teachers as Mr or Mrs or Miss followed by our surname. No one had called the Head 'Sir' since Victorian times.
Fortunately, Henry was a tall athletic boy, sufficiently self-possessed to ignore the stunned silence in the class and sufficiently able to look after himself in the playground to ensure any bullying was nipped in the bud.
Anyway, Henry would be going to boarding school at the end of the term so his stay with us would be quite brief.
'Good morning Mrs. A. I'm new here.' announced Henry as he greeted me on my first playground duty. He was a lively, intelligent conversationalist and my regular break time talks with him centred round his current main interests: natural history and maths.
He did have a vague interest in horses, one of my passions.
His aunt, Johanna Vardon, had established the National Foaling Bank.
Highly-strung thoroughbred mares sometimes reject their foals; they can attack or even kill them. Johanna took pity on the reject foals, carefully introducing them to a more maternal mare with the hope she would adopt them and bring them up as her own.
This took a great deal of time and expertise, as I found out. Sanyeh, my purebred Arab mare, had recently foaled. She hated Sherifah, the foal, on sight and wouldn't allow her to get near, let alone suckle.
Foals feed every two hours, including all through the night.

I couldn't cope with the night bottle-feeding, so in desperation I had contacted Johanna for help. She found a wonderful maternal mare to adopt Sherifah. After a couple of weeks the mare and newly adopted foal had bonded so well they could come home.

'Why do you think a mother would reject her young?' Henry asked. 'Doesn't she know it belongs to her? Do you think it is an unnatural act?' and off we would go on a discussion of maternal instincts, paternal reactions, and whether the uncaring non-maternal mare should be shot - or not, as the case may be.

Henry's other current interest was Maths. We enjoyed many rather one-sided conversations about Pythagoras, his life and loves, and his theorems. One-sided because my knowledge was 'O' level stuff, '…the square on the hypotenuse equals the sum of the squares on the other two sides' sort of thing.
Henry on the other hand had absorbed some interesting incidentals about Pythagoras.

'Did you know he was born on Samos?' he announced one day. 'Then he jumped island to Lesbos.' I had to admit I was ignorant on both those points. 'He got married at 60! Isn't that frightfully old?' I had to admit it seemed quite ancient to me. 'Her name was Theana.' He continued relentlessly, 'and he founded a school, and he was a member of a secret brotherhood – all connected with the science of maths. Don't you think that is really exciting and weird that maths should be secret?'
Yes, I thought it was.

'Pythagoras stayed in Egypt when he was young and studied pyramids. I would like to go to study pyramids…' his thoughts obviously wandered to triangles and squares, and the feat of engineering needed to build a pyramid. 'I want to study maths and maybe build a pyramid - would you like to come and help?' he asked.

I thought for a millisecond and hastily said
'Well Henry, I have to confess that pyramids are not my area of interest, neither, I regret to say, is the study of higher mathematics. However, there are people who are cleverer than I could ever be. Let's see who could point you in the right direction.' I made a mental note to contact the only other mathematician that I knew of in the village, the Vice Chairman of Lloyds Bank – he should be good at maths.

I took a breath and rang the bell to end playtime.

It was obvious that young Henry needed more challenging lessons than our village school was able to offer.

That afternoon Henry caused another sensation. He attended the maths class run by Mr. W, our head. I knew from conversations held over a cup of tea after school that Mr. W felt quite insecure in the realm of mathematics. He read carefully the Hertfordshire County Manual and conscientiously followed its advice on how to teach geometry, algebra, and numbers in the primary school. Unfortunately, he was not the type to say to a class

'Look. Wait. I need to look this up.'

Whereas that strategy had saved me, many a time.

It might have saved him if he had got Henry's measure and realised he had a bright enthusiastic maths expert in his class. As it was, he was well and truly caught out.

'Excuse me, Sir.' Came Henry's well-modulated voice from the back of the class, 'Excuse me Sir.'

Mr W sighed and turned. He was a little wary of Henry who he felt, quite rightly, was probably more knowledgeable than him in many areas.

'Yes, Henry.'

'Erm, there are three mistakes in your Algebra' said Henry 'May I show you?' He marched confidently to the front of the class and proceeded to correct a series of errors in the algebraic formula written up on the board.

The other children stared, open mouthed. No one was even moderately interested in algebra, and not one of them would have dared to correct Mr W even if they had noticed a mistake. But Henry had caught their attention. They gazed at him with awe. Would his temerity bring knobbly 'Old Missus' out of hibernation? 'Old Missus', the formidable cane, hard and gnarled, with a silver band near the top with her name beautifully engraved on it. She had been the pride and joy of some past headmaster but had not been used since the current pupils' parents had been at the school. Even then, she had been more of a threat than reality. If I explored the log books no doubt she would have featured large in the days when corporal punishment was the answer to everything.

However, much to some of the boys regret, the cane remained hidden at the back of the cupboard in my classroom. I rather think they were hoping for a demonstration!

Mr W looked at the board, looked at Henry and got out the HCC Manual. As he riffled through the pages, he could be heard muttering to himself. He stopped abruptly at the relevant page...

'Oh, right. Yes, possibly I wasn't concentrating, er, that y should be x and the x squared should be...he looked at the board again 'Yes yes, quite good.' He paused. Break time!' he announced, and quickly left the class to dismiss itself and get out to the playground.

He retired to his office and shut the door.

Everyone went out into the sunshine, except Henry who knocked on the door of my room.

'May I come in and finish that book on Egypt you found for me?' he asked, and settled himself comfortably into his accustomed desk in the corner.

Henry had publicly corrected the headmaster, and got away with it!

His status in eyes of the playground boys soared. Here was someone worthy of hero worship. Even the eleven year olds were impressed. He became a legend in the land – or anyway the village. Word went round that a genius had landed among us and interest in his family grew.

They had not been in the village long. Their house up Tom's Hill was opposite Millionaire's Row, an enclave of houses where men in black suits, from the city, had chosen their commutable residences. It was tacitly out of bounds for the likes of us.

The source of all knowledge of what went on, was a group of 'ladies that helped' in the larger houses.

The networking they managed was incredible. And infallible. It never took very long before all the important details about any new family were common village knowledge. Henry's parents were no exception.

They were relatively mature. His father had recently retired. It gradually became known that Sir James and Lady Barbara Bottomley had returned from South Africa where he had been Ambassador.

They had three children – Henry being the youngest, and were about to hold a soiree to introduce themselves to the villagers.

Cath Barber told me that I was to be invited, that I did not have to wear a long dress, that it was going to be informal and that flattish shoes would be a good idea as some of the guests might be shown round the garden. Of course, I took careful note, anxious to do the right thing.

When the official invitation arrived, it therefore came as no surprise. I was well prepared for my first foray into the world of politics and diplomacy.

The Bottomley's eldest son, Peter, and his wife Virginia, were both MPs, their sister, Susan, was a teacher.
Henry's future career was yet to be decided. However, he had confided in me that his favourite colour was 'red' whilst the family's was 'true blue'. If he entered the world of politics, it might well be on the opposite side of the House to his brother and sister in law.

The talk was mainly of village affairs, with Barbara being a perfect hostess, introducing every one and circulating in a manner that was very smooth and practised.
I did wonder if she was thinking of former ambassadorial occasions when, no doubt the guests were more eminent than a lowly schoolteacher, and the like. If she did, she gave no sign of it.

There was a sizable age gap between Henry and Peter.
I learnt later from Barbara that they had a son who had been tragically injured whilst on a school boating trip. Apparently, he had been told to sit down as the boat was coming to a low stone bridge, but either didn't hear or decided to ignore the order. He sustained a serious blow to his head, and died.
Not surprisingly, Henry was the apple of their eye.

He came to find me as I gazed through their French windows at their 'Ballerina' rose trees looking very like tutus-on-a-stick in tandem, leading down their undoubtedly pretty garden.
The windows were open and Henry was obviously eager to talk to me privately, so flat shoes at the ready we went out into the sweet smelling evening.

'There's going to be an election,' he announced as usual without any preamble. 'I'm going to help.' He managed to look both gleeful and mischievous at once.
I was immediately suspicious.

'What's in your head now, Henry you look positively evil.'

'Well,' he said 'the parents might not like it – but I do need your help – I need a reference as I am a bit young.'

He positively dragged me down the garden out of earshot of anyone in the house.

As he whispered in my ear his thoughts and ideas on the coming election, I decided to help him as I could not imagine his parents would have any objection to this early sign of political awareness. His plan was to help at the polling booth in the Memorial Hall at the forthcoming election. He would usher prospective voters into the hall.

I agreed to contact the local organiser for him

However, what he neglected to tell me was that he would sport a large red rosette on his lapel not the family's affiliation, blue.

My only contact with the political side of life at that time was a retired genteel little person called Miss Nellie Grange.

A small used-to-be-blonde, her powers of persuasion were phenomenal.

She was the local representative of the Conservative party and was renowned for her almost 100% recruitment in the village. Her methods were simple.

'It will cost you just one pound to join us.' she would announce to all and sundry.

She didn't care which party you actually voted for she just wanted to keep her membership list at its usual high level.

She trotted round the village knocking on doors, and talked at you until you found your pound and accepted a membership card, and then she would retreat triumphant!

No respecter of persons, or time of day - she invariably got her sub!

It was the custom in our village to leave all the doors unlocked. Most people would knock and wait to be invited in, but not Nellie. She walked in unannounced one day as my husband wandered down the stairs, stark naked after his shower. He was looking for a clean towel, because the cat had got into the airing cupboard again and had left hairs and half a mouse on top of my pile of fresh laundry.

He stood for a moment transfixed and then blushed to the top of his slightly bald head. Nellie remained in position, held out a Conservative party membership card and said reprovingly,

'Please may I have your pound? You are the last one to pay and I have to hand in my subscriptions at my meeting tomorrow.'

'Er, I don't have a pound on me just at the moment.' he replied, absently putting both hands down to where his trouser pockets would have been had he been wearing any. He then turned and raced upstairs, thoroughly unnerved. I followed slowly, gesturing to Nellie to stay where she was.

'For God's sake give her the pound' he hissed at me from the haven of our bedroom. 'DON'T offer her tea. Get rid of her.'

I found my purse and came down stairs feeling embarrassed on her behalf. After all, she was a spinster lady.

I needn't have worried.

She accepted our pound, gracefully handed out a pre-written receipt and smiled slightly as she turned to go.

'Your husband is… erm, a fine figure of a man.' she said with a twinkle in her eye, 'make sure he doesn't catch a chill.' With that perfect exit line she closed our front door softly behind her, and left I was so non-plussed I had forgotten to ask her about Henry and the imminent hustings, so now I would be subject to a one-sided, protracted phone call in order to make the arrangements for him.

Nellie would be pleased she had her full complement of members again this year!

The time came when Henry was due to leave us, the summer holidays were almost upon us he would be off to his new school. He came to say goodbye.

I felt really sad to lose my stimulating playground conversationalist, but I promised I would take an interest in his progress, hoping for news about him from his mother.

'You didn't tell me about that red rosette you wore, did you? I teased him. 'I hope your parents weren't too cross.'

'Oh no.' he replied blithely, 'Mother says it's interesting that various members of our family support various Parties – and Margaret Thatcher got in anyway, so my brother was safe. I just wanted to be a bit…independent. This is for you.' He added, handing me a thick piece of knotted twine, 'I hope it will remind you of what we talked about. Goodbye and thank you.'

He shook my hand, turned, and walked down the path by the privet hedge disappearing up Toms Hill, towards his house.

I examined the piece of string Henry had given me. It had twelve evenly spaced knots in it. It was about two feet long.

'What on earth is this for…? Maybe a necklace…?' I mused, and then I remembered.
Pyramid building.

'Of course, this is what those early followers of Pythagoras had used to measure their right angled triangle, so necessary for the building of pyramids.
How very thoughtful of him.
Not to be put off by my lack of enthusiasm for his project he clearly hoped to see a teacher-built designer pyramid somewhere in the village, enhancing its old world charm.
The problem was, as I just couldn't think of a suitable place, I am sorry to report the village still awaits its first Pythagorean pyramid. Perhaps Henry…?

****

Henry eventually got a position at Lloyds Bank where he stayed for about a year before moving on to enter politics, on the other side of the House, to write books, invent number conundrums, to get married, and eventually find his niche as a statistician with the former DTI.
(See Henry's web page.) His niece, Catherine Ussher who I also taught briefly, entered Parliament too.
An interesting, and exceedingly talented family.
I was glad to have known them.

Clive's Dig

'Hitler you're barmy,
You went to join the army,
Got knocked out by a bottle of stout,
Hitler you're barmy.

R.A.F. o'er Berlin
Dropping bombs in play,
Hitler in his shelter
Shouts hip hip hooray.'

Lewisham, London S.E.13, 1940s

I had fallen in love with the small village school as soon as I saw it. The building was Victorian red brick with arched diamond-paned windows. Its front door would not have looked out of place in a mediaeval church.

Living in the village as I did, I met members of the school everywhere I went, in the shop where one of the mums was postmistress, or riding my bike along the lane to the pond to feed the ducks.
Sometimes I met a gaggle of giggling girls who might offer me a sweet from a crumpled and definitely grubby bag, or I could be sitting under the old elm where Charles Wesley was supposed to have preached when faces would often peer round its knobbly trunk, usually smiling shyly at me.

I was ambling down to the Post Office one sunny afternoon when three rather dishevelled boys approached me with the guiltiest looks you could ever see on ten-year-old faces.

'Afternoon Clive, Robert, Stephen.' said I, nodding to each in turn, 'Where have you been, you look a bit out of breath? Have you been running?'

'No miss.' they chorused. 'We've been… in the rec.'

The recreation field was up by my house, I had just come from there. I had seen no sign of them.

'H'm…,' I said rather surprised, 'you look thirsty, fancy a drink of orange?'

They eagerly accepted and as I doled out the paper cups I kept with my bottle of orange I had a chance to look at them closely.

Just William and his gang wasn't in it… these three would have graced a Richmal Crompton tale with ease. They all looked bulky, pockets bulging with treasures, and Clive's looked quite heavy.

'What have you got, boys?' I added, 'Have you found something interesting? Anything we can share with our class?' Clive, the ringleader, opened his mouth to tell me but just then his mother Doris came by with their scruffy but very loveable Heinz of a dog, Rinty.

'What are you doing, bothering your teacher? Get yourself home for your tea, you're late. It's on the table.' With that, she trotted off up the road to the rec. where she regularly went to have a quiet, illicit smoke behind the cricket shed.

As one they turned and headed down to Clive's house without a goodbye or backward glance.

'Shame.' I thought. 'Bad timing, Doris.'

As a new teacher I would have liked to win Clive over, gain his trust. I had hoped my confidence-winning opportunity had arrived just then. He was a born leader and although a scamp of the first water I had grown to admire his qualities. Where he went the rest of the class would follow, and I wanted to gain their interest and attention. Already I felt the protective instinct about the progress of 'my' children evolving. It seemed to grow as time went on and as our relationship strengthened.

My class was housed in what was known as 'The Hut'. It was a prefabricated building of uncertain age situated at the back of the main solidity of the Victorian building. We liked the togetherness the slight isolation seemed to foster. The views from the windows were of beautiful fields, woods and the next-door farm. All was conducive to peace, quiet, and intensive learning!

'Good morning everyone, it's news time – has anyone anything to tell us?' I asked as they all settled down after their half term break.. We were hoping to generate a class journal so each day we had a 'report to the editor' session. Clive was the editor.

Various children came forward with bits of news. Mary's Mum had had her baby at home and not in the hospital.

'He came out so quick,' Mary said, 'did you know they're all mucky when they come. His name's Dave...' She didn't get a chance to finish as all the class went 'Ugh' in unison.

'Yes, of course they do.' I interjected. 'Don't you remember when Paul's Dad's cow had her calf? All newborn mammals are covered in lubricant.'

Somewhat above their heads that, but I didn't want to delve into human reproduction processes just then.

One of the 'Gang of Three', Robert, brought an unidentified metal object to the front of the class. He held it up proudly.

'We found the army treasure trove.' he announced. 'We dug and dug and we found lots of stuff ...' he trailed off at Clive's fulminating glare. Gathering nerve he went on, 'It's an enormous bullet. Empty though.' He added the last with real regret.

I inspected it closely. It was about a foot long and looked like a dirty version of the polished brass specimens of used shell cases you sometimes see in antique shops.

'Great, you can write about how you found it and we'll go to the library and see if we can identify it.'

He didn't look exactly thrilled at the idea. Finding and keeping were good: reading and writing were work!

'What's the problem Clive? Have you got something to show us?' My question only made Clive look more resentful. He muttered something to Stephen who came forward nervously holding a handful of dirty metallic objects, flat at one end and pointed at the other. Every eye, including mine, focused on Stephen's hand. 'Better put those on my desk Stephen,' I said, 'just in case they're dangerous.'

To me they looked like a handful of bullets for a rather large gun. I knew nothing about firearms but resolved to do some research later.

'My cat had five kittens last night Miss' said Rosie out of the blue, patently not interested in the dirty findings of grubby boys. 'Can I write about it now please?' she asked. Our editor's moment was over and it was time to go on to other things in our busy school schedule.

In light of the fact I was suspicious of the Gang of Three's activities and extremely curious as to where they had found the warlike artefacts I mentally reserved ten minutes of playtime to chat to Clive. I knew he had something to hide.

I was listening to reading when he came up to me holding an oval shaped object. It was rather like an oversized dirty brownish egg with bits at one end.

'Will you look after this for me Miss?' he asked 'It's digging into me leg.' I gave it a cursory glance.

'Put it on my table and come to me at playtime.' I suggested. As I was fully occupied with teaching this multi-skilled, challenging class, I took little notice of the object reposing on my desktop.

Clive and I met as arranged. The other children streamed out into the spring-warm air to play.

'Well! First of all, where did you find this?' I asked. Clive countered with,

'Promise you won't tell my Mum, miss?' His tone was a mix of command and entreaty. I considered the question. I knew he would tell me if I promised: I was not so sure if I declined. But I had to be honest with him.

'Clive, I can't keep secrets from your Mum. I am really sorry.' I looked him in the eye. His gaze never faltered as he made up his mind. My heart sank. Silence.

Then with a deep breath, he came out with his story.

'We went up to the dump, up Tom's Hill and into the woods. You can find all sorts there, clay pipes, old bottles with marbles in the lids, some made from stone. Lots of army things are buried there too. That's where we found this stuff.'

'Well, let's look at what you've have brought us.' Wonder how it got there I mused. He picked it up. It was definitely a hand grenade, not that I had ever seen one, but many war films showed them. The Dirty Dozen had been filmed up there, indeed during my first day in my house I had seem streams of tanks going past the front garden manned by American soldiers. It was a great relief to discover they were only part of a film shoot and not my new neighbours!

We examined the soil-covered object.

'It's cleaner than it was, I carried it in my pocket for a couple of days and put it under my pillow at night so Mum didn't find it.'

Clive volunteered this information rather defiantly.

I made no comment. I was beginning to feel decidedly uneasy. Surely the end was pulled out when they threw it? There were bits still stuck in, like two rings. I wondered if it was a prop for the war film. I picked a bullet from the pile sitting on my desk and looked at it closely. How do you tell whether it has been fired from the gun - or not? I looked at Clive.

'You know I must find out a bit more about the things you have found I think we had better ask the Head to come and have a look. What do you think?'

'Oh gawd, Mum'll have a fit.' he replied.

I hid a grin and said gravely,

'I really am sorry but we don't exactly know what they are, do we?'

The Head took a close look at the array of objects on my desk.

'I think we had better give Ted a call.' he said. Ted was the local policeman.

He was large, comforting and knowledgeable. He took one look at the army left-overs on my desk and said in a completely different voice from his usual calm deep, slow delivery, '

Why don't we get you all up the road into the Playgroup hall? Really FAST!' he commanded.

The whole school left the premises with the Headteacher.

I stayed with Ted who then rang the bomb disposal unit. When I described to them what lay on my desk they instructed Ted and me to leave the premises at once and meet them at a safe distance from the school.

We decided the duck pond at the bottom of Tom's Hill was far enough away from any danger.

The army landrover came down the hill at a rate of knots and screeched to a halt near us as we stood on the verge.

Ted and one of the soldiers in the army Land Rover conferred, just out of earshot. Ted went rather white.

'Go up to the playgroup, wait there until further instructions.' said Ted.

I began to argue the point – after all it was my pupil's hand grenade, but after a quick look at the soldier's face decided to do as I was instructed.

Half an hour later Ted arrived at the entrance to the hall.

'They've taken everything away to investigate and will report their results to us, later.' he announced.

Clive, in the meantime, was the centre of attention. All the children clustered round the 'Gang of Three' whispering excitedly and Clive was to be heard nonchalantly saying,

'Oh I've got lots more at home…'

With that Ted looked meaningfully at me, took out his walkie-talkie and began muttering into it.

We eventually returned to school, back to the mundane prospect of lessons, although it was quite difficult to concentrate on maths. My desk was comfortingly devoid of any military remains. Clive was unnaturally quiet.

At home time, he came to me with the air of a conspirator,

'You won't tell Mum nothing, now, will you?' I thought of the army and felt able to say

'No, the soldiers will take care of everything.'

Later that evening Ted appeared at my front door.

'I thought you'd like to know. All that stuff was from World War Two. Capt. Smith went to Clive's house and searched his bedroom. He had a brown paper carrier full of bullets, empty shells, a few badges and another grenade. His Mum went into hysterics.' He finished, 'I d've wrung his neck…'

Apparently, the grenade Clive had tenderly cared for under his pillow was live. If it had exploded it could have blown his head off and killed or maimed anyone who was near him.

The bullets were also live. The overall explosion would have made a sizeable crater.'

He paused. I felt a little nauseous.

'Clive, of course, is the hero of the hour.' He added. 'When I last saw him, he was ambling down the street surrounded by his mates, all proffering various bribes to be shown where the army dump was. He had refused to tell Capt Smith in spite of his attempts at persuasion saying the only one worth telling was his teacher. He would take her there any day.'

I suppose I felt flattered.

The army had arranged with Ted to come on to the school football field to illustrate the extent of the crater that would have appeared had the grenade and bullets exploded. The circle they outlined with a rope seemed to cover about half the field. Clive and his friends had brought, albeit unwittingly, live ammunition in my class of 20 or so children and had endangered life and limb of everyone. The army hammered home the disastrous effect on all of us if that grenade and the bullets had exploded. It hardly bore thinking about. No wonder Clive's mother had hysterics. I was quite near it myself and even phlegmatic Ted had changed colour!

'What was the Ministry of Defence thinking of?' I fumed, 'Why hadn't they cleared the site and made it safe after the War?'

'These things get forgotten at the time there was so much to clear up.' said Ted soothingly, 'By the way, Capt. Smith will be along to see you tomorrow after your chat with Clive.' Ted continued to my dismay,
'He wants you to be the one to give him a guided tour of the Dump. He has organised a 'dig' to make sure there is nothing else left to surprise us!'
He grinned at me when he saw my face.
'Don't worry, the Army doesn't let civilian personnel take unnecessary risks.'

'Oh no, I suppose not...' I stammered.
In the past I had often wandered there myself, with my dogs, in search of the old glass bottles.
 Now I knew the hazards I gulped as I wondered if there were such things as bombproof boots, or trousers, or jackets available in my size. Just in case. Stepping on a live grenade by mistake would definitely be living dangerously, but not my kind of adventure, I thought.
All of a sudden, I had a great admiration for the people who disabled unexpected bombs in unfriendly places as part of their everyday duties. What a rotten, scary job.
I was so glad to be only a teacher.

****

Clive was probably the most enterprising lad I ever taught.
His life was filled with 'adventures' like running from one end of Trooper Road to the Trooper Pub without touching the ground using

the tops of cars as stepping stones. He opened the formidable locked front door of our school with my hair clip (picking the lock with ease) that time it had slammed shut with the wind, locking us all out in the playground. He tried sitting on a theatre balcony only to fall precipitately on to the surprised row of people below him… and many other adventures I can't even remember. I thought he was fabulous!

He is now married to Tracy, with wonderful children who look remarkably like him and seem to be growing up just like him.

I do hope so.

Shillingbury Tales
or
My first TV Appearance

'Patience is a virtue,
Virtue is a grace…
Go and ask your mother to wash your dirty face.'

Old saying in our family... 1942

''The village of Shillingbury is a tranquil place, staunch to the old fashioned values of rural England. It is a picture postcard place of honeysuckle and home-made strawberry jam, teas, fine thatched roofs, a timbered pub and contented folk…
Peopled with quaint characters like Cuffy the Tinker, Peter and Sally, the newcomers, and Jake the local farmer. It is a rural idyll.''
I couldn't have put it better myself. The scene is set for yet another TV production about to invade the real life of our village.
Nestling at the foot of the soft rolling Chiltern Hills, it is true; Aldbury *is* very pretty, with its duck pond in the middle, overlooked by magnificent Ashridge Forest. A seat surrounds its large tree on the green, mediaeval stocks, which originally restrained wrongdoers, still stand nearby. The ancient church, the Victorian school, the Greyhound Pub and the village shop are all within a step or two of the centre.
People in the village are divided into two main groups, 'The Locals', who have lived there for generations and 'The Incomers' of only a few years standing. Locals just about put up with us Incomers.
Although woe-betide anyone who contravenes established village customs.
Like newly arrived Micky Ridgway, he was definitely an Incomer with outlandish ideas. He was also a Cambridge graduate, inventor, singer morris dancer, bell ringer…, who felt the pond needed a facelift.

Lless-than-pristine water ran down Toms Hill every time it rained, feeding directly into our pond, which was quite overgrown with rushes and pondweed.

To an eye untutored in rural ways, it looked a bit of an eyesore. Taking matters into his own hands, and consulting no one, Micky was caught wet-handed by an Old Inhabitant early one morning. Wearing waders, and up to his thighs in murky water, he had decided to clear out most of the weed and plant several beautiful water lilies. Old Inhabitant was incensed.

Outrage against the townie interfering b**** echoed and re-echoed round the Chiltern Hills.

It took several years for the 'pond man' to re establish his credibility after *that* liberty. It wasn't until he became a bell ringer and a leading light of the Morris dancers, that he was really forgiven, and even then some muttered. Locals liked the pond as it was, in its natural untouched-by-human hand state.

Fortunately, our ducks were not so critical; they simply relished the unexpected addition to their diet. It took only a matter of days for the pond to revert to its rural state of murky water, a few tadpoles who had escaped the ducks' ever-exploring beaks, and thick silt round the edge with stubby rushes, like a bristling moustache.

The locals' resentment then showed only in occasional over-the-bar caustic comments at The Trooper, the locally preferred village pub along Trooper Road.

Whenever filming took place, the crew attracted considerable attention from the schoolchildren. The novelty of roadblocks, TV stars, and bits of naturalistic scenery strategically placed here and there was irresistible. They raced out en masse, each day after school, to see what was happening next.

Roads were closed without notice.

Pillars of the community, anxious to get to work, were abruptly stopped in their tracks when a scene was being shot.

In vain, the monitors of the shoot exhorted passersby to

'Be still and be silent – we are shooting a scene,' or 'this road will be closed for an hour, please turn and go the other way.' Expletives could be heard from open car windows, and truculent local farmers on tractors were known to ignore any plea for silence and just trundled on though the set as if it wasn't there.

The eminent director kept his thoughts to himself about the cost of re-takes.

In the summer months, I rode my bicycle down Stocks Road, to school. It was an ancient steed with a wicker basket on the front and sit-up and beg handlebars. With my satchel flapping wildly full of the previous night's marking, and my wide-brimmed sunhat I must have looked 'local' indeed.

One morning two earphone-laden men waved me down.

'Stop! Are you the village school teacher?' they demanded.

'Don't you dare stop me now, I am late for my class,' I snapped 'I've no time to linger…' and I started to pedal even harder. One of the men ran alongside me, somewhat hampered by his recording gear.

'Wait! We need an extra, will you be in the film? Stop! We need to talk to you.'
I stopped in my tracks.

'Me? Are you sure it's *me* you want?'

'Are you the village school teacher?' they repeated. I nodded. 'Well, yes it's you we've been told to find.'

'I *really* can't stop now but I'll come after school.' I shouted at them over my shoulder, as I fast tracked down the road, again.

'OK then, meet us in the Memorial Hall at 3.30…'
The day passed in a blur. Visions of stardom flashed past my eyes, Trevor Howard was in this production and Robin Nedwell too. Maybe I would be in a scene with them. I could hardly wait for home time.

After school, followed by a few loyal members of my class anxious to see their teacher's meteoric rise to stardom, I parked my bike outside the Hall and found my two film crew drinking coffee and eating bacon sandwiches. Their ever-open canteen van was the envy of the villagers. The seductive smell of frying bacon combined with freshly ground coffee began to waft over the village green from six am, making everyone who passed, feel hungry. They were talking reverentially to a shortish man in a blue summer shirt.

'Here I am' I announced interrupting their flow. The man in the blue shirt looked me up and down in a disinterested sort of a way, and said

'OK, she'll do.'

And that was it. Val Guest, the Director, had approved me. I was hired.

'We'll take you to Make-up and she will tell you when to report for your scene. You have to be available the whole day, you know.' I hoped the Head, Mr W, wouldn't mind me missing school, although I was past caring by that time, as visions of a new career floated round my brain.

'I'm Make-up.' said a slightly harassed looking female busy touching up the face of a dark haired, pretty woman seated in the chair at her side. 'Who are you?' – She directed a searching look at me. The woman in the chair got up to go.

'Thank you Miss Keen, you'll need a re-touch later'.

I was thrilled to recognise Diane Keen the star of the film, who gave me an absent smile as she strolled away.

I made as if to sit down in the chair.

'Hey' said a male voice from behind 'wait, are you teacher?' As I turned to look at him he added

'I'm Props, where is it?'

'I'm teacher, where is what?' Their style of speech was catching.

'The horse of course!' he replied. My little entourage giggled.

'What are you talking about, what horse?'

'Don't you keep horses? We were told you keep horses, we need a horse.' He looked at his clipboard, 'We're shooting tomorrow, 8 am. We need a horse for then. I was told this is the real 'countryfied England',' he muttered irritably, 'everyone's got a horse.'

'And a rider.' added Make-up.

They confirmed they wanted a horse and rider to take part in the film. The horse had to be a pretty colour. They didn't seem to care much about the rider's looks.

I had been chosen because one of my class, chatting with one of the crew, had told them his teacher kept horses.

I imagined me intrepidly galloping round the pond, a la John Wayne, my trusty steed ready to leap into the water at a moment's notice or even riding hell for leather down Stocks Road like Paul Revere.

Still, I hesitated. It was a great deal of work to bring a horse in from the field, shampoo the dust off his coat, brush it to a shine, wash mane and tail and present him to a suitable standard for appearing on film.

'We will pay you £100 per hour' said Props perhaps a little recklessly. The entourage gasped. So did I. That was quite a lot of money.

'OK,' I instantly decided 'You've got me - and my horse. What time do you want us?'

Make-up told me they started at 6 am so I had better be there then in case any adjustments had to be made.

I rode my bike home faced with an evening's hard work of cleaning saddle, bridle, horse, and me. Husband would do children's supper.

I would eat on the hoof. The possibility of a career change was fading, but I was extremely excited all the same. I spent my £100 several times over, before finally deciding on a special luxury holiday, or maybe a visit to Champneys Health resort situated a couple of miles away.

Perhaps I could register as a film extra and make a small fortune hiring Lou, my horse, and myself out at a premium fee.

Lou, was a Purebred Arab gelding. His studbook entry read 'Ludraz: Sire Radfan…Dam Ludoette' But we all called him Lou. He had a rich chestnut coat with a silky strawberry blonde mane and tail, typical of the breed.

His eyes were large and expressive and his ears curled slightly inwards at the tips somehow giving him a quizzical expression. Everyone who made contact with him loved him; he was such a great softie, especially with children.

His main vice was mud bathing. Finding any patch of mud in the field he would lie down, roll onto his back and grind the mud into his fur. It stuck like plaster to a wall, with great lumps attaching themselves to his mane. He loved it. I groaned as I brought him into his box that evening. He was covered. The recent rain had provided several ideal places for him to indulge in his favourite pastime. It usually took a good couple of hours to hose him down, shampoo him all over, and then dry him with thick towels in order for me to brush him thoroughly.

A great deal of effort was needed to restore the shine to his coat. I used anti-tangle spray on his mane and tail so I could comb them out easily. My work was cut out if he was to be beautiful for his film debut. At a quarter to midnight, I surveyed my handiwork. He was covered from rump to ears in a soft night rug, shaped to fit him closely. His tail was covered with one leg of a pair of my nylon tights so that it would retain its smooth appearance should he decide that his wood-shaving bedding would also be a good place to roll.

I had worked on his appearance as if he was to take part in the showing class in the prestigious Arab Horse Society Annual Show, held at Ascot. I was exhausted. My own hair was as long as Lou's tail, so I thought I had better give it a quick wash too, before I tumbled into bed.

The alarm clock woke me at five o'clock. It took me ten minutes to dress in my riding trousers, boots, riding shirt, grab a cup of coffee along with my black velvet riding hat and scoot to the yard. Lou, bless his cotton socks, was standing looking sleepily out at the sunny early morning with wisps of hay hanging from the corner of his mouth.

His protective gear was still in place so all I had to do was take it all off, give him a cursory polish with the silk scarf I kept for the purpose, oil his hooves, pick out his feet, brush some white chalk into his snow white socks, put on his bridle and saddle him up. He was ready.

It was a quarter to six so I just jumped on board and trotted smartly out of the quiet yard, without checking in any mirror hoping Make-up would use her skills to make me presentable too.

I felt proud of us both when we arrived as all the crew stopped eating their breakfast and turned to look admiringly at us.

Make-up and Props came bustling over to meet me.

I dismounted, ready to be shown to Make-up's chair.

She didn't even glance my way.

'Isn't he beautiful,' she breathed 'what a fabulous colour. I love his tail…' and she produced a brush and comb that looked remarkably like the ones she had used on Diane Keen the previous evening.

She began to gently brush Lou's tail. He loved it. Like most show horses, he was used to admiration and took it all as his due. He stood like a statue as she fussed around him using brush and comb on his mane and forelock.

He fluttered his eyelashes at her and did his trick of gently resting his head on her shoulder and breathing softly into her ear, his usual sign of appreciation.

'Don't move!' She instructed me 'I want to take a picture.' And she rushed off to get her camera.

Props stood there with his clip board.

'Right we've got horse.' He muttered, proceeding to tick off various items on his very long list.

'And rider,' I prompted brightly 'and rider.'

He turned away without reply and went briskly over to another group of extras, pencil moving as he walked.

I could smell bacon and coffee. Everyone was eating, drinking and talking to each other. I stood holding the reins, with Lou placidly nibbling at the grass on the Green.

I was starving having had no supper to speak of and no breakfast. I could hear a dull rumble in my stomach.

One of the men wearing earphones jumped and looked at me sharply.

'Sorry.' I mouthed 'I'm hungry.'

The wonderful man went to the counter and came over to me with a steaming coffee cup and a sandwich in a serviette.

Make-up appeared with her camera.

'Stand back I don't need you.' She said to me as her camera clicked several times in quick succession. Lou lifted his head and looked straight at her.

'Oh boy, what a marvellous shot…'

I am not sure how long I would have been left standing there but Robin and Diane, the stars, appeared with Trevor Howard, who was in the next take.

The atmosphere changed, everyone became exceedingly busy: the working day had begun.

Lou and I were moved to stand beside the pond. Diane Keen, who seemed a bit nervous, was asked to stand by Lou for some stills.

'Don't worry – he loves having his photo taken, he will stand like a rock.' I murmured to her.

However, as soon as the photo shoot was over she moved smartly away and I was left in splendid isolation again.

I heard the church clock strike nine. The children on their way to school came to pat and stroke Lou, who ignored them; they smiled at me as they ran past.

A few older boys were hurriedly eating bacon sandwiches and some of the little girls seemed to be stuffing forbidden sweets into their pockets.

The film crew were extremely generous to the local children, although Mr W. had forbidden them to bring edibles into school.

By then, though, I was getting extremely bored. The filming was taking place down Stocks Road outside Rose Cottage, temporary home to Peter and Sally (Robin and Diane) 'the incomer' characters in the film.

I couldn't see anything, I was just left standing.

I was tethered to Lou, as he couldn't be left on his own.

He too, was getting bored. He showed this by walking round in circles, fiddling with his bit, and trying to nibble any part of me he could reach.

He'd had enough of grass, photos, and adulation. He wanted a drink, and he wanted his usual ride up the hill into the woods, where he knew we would have a trot and a canter, which he loved. I took him to the edge of the pond and allowed him his drink.

Unfortunately, his ironclad hooves clip-clopped on the short length of road, as we made our way there.

'CUT, CUT' yelled an annoyed voice from outside the cottage. 'Who the hell let a horse loose… we'll have to do a re-take.'

'Oh dear,' muttered a voice in my ear from one of the other extras, 'that'll cost a packet. Trevor is in this scene – he's very expensive.'

With that he walked away anxious not to be associated with me and Lou – the only horse for miles.

Make-up and Props appeared looking very busy.

'Keep that horse quiet.' ordered Props.

I needed to talk to Make-up. I had dressed very hurriedly that morning, thinking that I would be gone over and groomed when I arrived. I was keen to have some pink lipstick on at the very least…

Make-up inspected Lou again.

'He's poohed.' she said accusingly 'His tail needs a clean.'

A diet of fairly rich grass does things to the horse's digestion she didn't want to know about – all outgoings are deep green and quite 'loose' as we would say in the horse world.

His newly washed, silky blond tail looked distinctly green round the lower edges. It would need at the very least a wet wipe-over.

Make-up handed me a large towel.

'You deal with it, he's your horse.'

She hurried away over to one of the other extras

The kind man with the earphones came over with a large flask of warm water from the coffee urn. I was very grateful as a cold-water douche would not have pleased my rather sensitive Lou.

I soaked the towel with water, wiped his tail clean and popped the towel in the Tesco's bag thoughtfully provided by Earphones, and handed him back the bag.

He took it without a word, and put it in the canteen rubbish bin standing by the van.

'It *is* boring,' he remarked on his return, 'all the waiting around. In this world every minute counts and they don't want to be hunting for loose extras when they are ready to shoot. I'll bring you some lunch, don't worry.

Why don't you sit ON your horse, so that you are ready?'

I had long given up hoping for Make-up to make me lovely, so his offer of a leg up was very welcome.

As I settled myself in the saddle, Props came back.

'Five minute call.' He said – 'I thought I'd let you know early, but you will be told when to go.'

'Go where?' I shouted at him, but he was already out of earshot.

I had absolutely no idea what I was supposed to be doing.

The cameras, lots of men wearing earphones, Props, Make-up and a car with a camera mounted on the roof all came down towards me. Suddenly we were surrounded with equipment, the car, and people all talking quite loudly to each other.

Lou didn't like it.

We were hemmed in on all sides.

He started doing his on-the-spot trot, a preamble to an attempt at taking off at a rate of knots.

He was thoroughly upset.

'Stand back, give us room or you might have very damaged equipment...' I shouted.

Lou had never kicked out in his life but there was always a first time. Everyone, except the car did a quick back track.

'Let's get this scene rolling.' called an unidentified voice

'Cameras... Sound.' And there was a whirr from the man on the roof of the car.

We were being filmed.

I had no idea where to go.

'Move.' hissed Props.

'CUT - FOR GOD'S SAKE SHUT UP.' Yelled the same annoyed voice as before.

'SILENCE.'

I decided to go forward, quite smartly as Lou wanted a good gallop but reining him in firmly we managed a sedate –ish trot down Stocks Road, past the edge of the pond.

I followed the slow moving camera car as it crawled along in front of us, preventing any faster pace.

'CUT.' Yelled the voice.

The cameraman on top of the car, who was about level with my chest, told me to go back and do it all again.

We repeated that exercise at least half a dozen times. Each time there was a either an unwanted voice, a bicycle coming by, or a tractor driven by one of those farmers deaf to instructions from film crews. I was heartily sick of the whole idea.

There was obviously no prospect of galloping up Stocks Road, no riding like John Wayne and no paddling in the pond.

Lou and I were in total agreement, it was extremely *boring*.

On my return to the pond for the umpteenth time, there was a message to one of the ear-phoned men.

'Fine,' he said to me 'that last take is fine. You can go home. We'll be in touch.'

'When will I see myself on film?' I asked eagerly.

He looked at me pityingly 'No idea, we might not even use it.'

'Oh… well…, 'bye then.' But by then he had another voice in his ear and wasn't even looking.

I couldn't see Earphone, the food and drink man, so I never did say 'Thanks for saving my life.'

Turning Lou homeward we trotted so fast stable-wards that we struck sparks from the tarmac.

Visions of green field and mud patch filled Lou's head. Bath, supper and TV filled mine.

I was definitely *not* going to change from my interesting, demanding teaching job to a boring role in films.

Not for even if I was offered £1,000 a go!

****

When Shillingbury Tales was finally shown on ITV, I was on tenterhooks.

I still didn't know if I was in it.

The music started and the camera showed a bird's eye view of this stunning village with its pond, and idyllic country roads.

However the plump rump of a chestnut horse gently swinging its silky strawberry blonde tail glinting in the sunlight and the plump rump of its rider with a gently swinging ponytail of strawberry blonde hair moving slowly past the pond were nowhere to be seen.

Instead, a long shot of a smartly trotting chestnut horse and rider appeared for an instant as they scooted across the screen before the scene changed and the story began.

With a shock, I recognised Lou and me. We *were* in it!

'Quick, I'm on TV!' I shrieked to my family but by the time they all rushed in the moment had gone - and so had we.

My blast of glory had lasted about 10 seconds.

My concern about my shirt hanging out, my lack of attention from Make-up, my boring day suddenly didn't matter.

I was IN A FILM. Thousands of people would see my chance of a lifetime.

Although I realised, with due humility, It wasn't me they really wanted at all, it was my pretty, chestnut horse with his quizzical look, blond mane and long silky blond tail. He was the one with charisma and star appeal.

Oh, well I suppose I knew my place, groom, feed supplier, washer of tails, provider of thick clean beds... if it hadn't been for Lou I would never have been even a 10 second TV star at all.

The DVD 'Shillingbury Tales' can be obtained from Amazon – I really am in it!

Pigs in my Poke

'This little pig went to market,
This little pig stayed at home,
...This little pig cried 'Wee wee wee...'

The Nurse's Song, circa 1728

During our class discussions about an Adventure Club, several of the children had asked me to take them to visit our Yard, behind our house in Stocks Road where we kept a variety of animals, mainly for the joy of looking after them!
'We're not coming. We're not 'girly'.' asserted most of the boys scornfully, its sissy to play with horses and the like.
One of the attractions for the girls was the pair of yard cats we had recently been given by the Cat Rescue Society in Hemel Hempstead. Cats were definitely a working asset at any Yard, as they helped to keep the mice population, and the odd rat, to a minimum.
However, in the end when the time came I had a full complement of pupils.
'We don't want to miss anything,' explained Clive. 'We want to meet your Vietnamese Potbelly pigs.'
So one evening after school, we found ourselves assembled in the middle of our yard, sitting around on straw bales, snack bags open with some children munching on their pre-supper sustenance.
'Say hallo to Heidi' called Janet-the helper, as she led our much-loved nanny goat along the short passageway between the barns into the middle of the yard.
We could hear the patter of tiny hooves before the explosion of Heidi, the mother, and her four little six-week-old kids rounded the corner.
The kids LOVED visitors.

They rushed up to each child in turn and before anyone knew it, the snack packs, jackets, bags and contents were scattered all round us as the children vainly tried to protect their belongings.

'Look Mrs A, look,' Elaine called 'it's on my lap... ouch' she squealed as the over enthusiastic kid tugged at her hair, in an effort to attract her attention.

Janet carried on past us, leading Heidi to her loose box at the end of the row where she and her babies spent the night. An enticing feed of barley and hay awaited her so she almost dragged Janet along in her eagerness to get there first. Although the kids were still suckling, they got their noses in any bucket lying around at every opportunity.

So, in spite of interest in the children and their belongings the 'four musketeers' skidded past the front of the loose boxes, past the interested heads of the horses overlooking the scene and into the stable at the end with the bucket of food.

Heidi lost that race, but as she knew her feed would be replaced later, she resignedly allowed the kids to finish the small amount of barley in the bucket and got herself stuck into the hay.

'Wow,' exclaimed Philip C 'will the pigs be like that?'

'No, of course not,' I reassured him. 'don't worry; goat kids are famous for their naughtiness. You were lucky they only ate one snack, and it has rained for a while!

We had a very smart visitor here last week,' I went on to tell them, 'with a beautiful polished white car. He was dressed in cream trousers and a pale blue shirt. Heidi was tethered there,' I pointed a little way up the field. 'Her kids were playing around here, just where we are now. The man parked near where you're standing Philip, and got out of his car and left the door open.' I paused. 'You'll never guess what...'

Patrick interjected, a little bitterly.

'They stole his lunch?' All that was left of *his* snack pack was a crumpled empty bag discarded by a sneaky marauding goat kid.

'No,' I said 'worse; for him anyway. Two of them jumped inside his car, got very excited and leapt out with some of his papers in their mouths throwing them around as they went. The other two jumped on the bonnet and onto the ROOF!'

The children looked fascinated.

'I suppose that wouldn't have been too bad, but if you remember it had rained and the gateway to the field is quite muddy. They had all squeezed under the bars of the gate…'

'Oh dear,' said Vicky, a neat little blonde girl, 'I bet the mud stuck to their fur. I bet the papers got dirty.'

'Oh yes! The pale cream seats were muddied all over as well, and the roof of the car was COVERED in hoof prints. Sixteen feet can make quite a mess. The man saw all this from our kitchen window and rushed out shouting, as he ran

'Gerroff, gerroff you little… so and so's!'
The kids thought it was great fun, two leapt on the bonnet and then joined the others on the roof, dancing from one side to the other as he ran round the car trying in vain to catch them.'

'I bet he said some bad words,' Robin observed wisely, 'My Dad cleans his car every week and gets cross if we even lean our bikes against it.'

'I can understand that, cleaning cars by hand is jolly hard work.' I continued, 'My husband came out after the man and asked him if he would like to go back to the house for a cloth to clean up.

'Oo-oh no, I'm off.' he said, muttering something to himself about owners of pets who have no discipline… The kids had got tired by then and had melted away.
'I bet he never comes back!' I said. You know, I never actually found out what he had come for.'
I thought of the impact that sixteen little muddy hooves would have made on the pristine upholstery and the rub-off effect on his pale trousers and blue shirt, and grinned to myself.
'That would teach him to come to the country in ridiculous townie clothes!' said my husband in my ear as we cheerfully waved to the scowling driver half way out of the drive in about half a second.

'Who wants to come and meet Rosy and Rolo our new kittens?' asked Janet, 'they are black and white bundles of fur at the moment. Rolo caught his first mouse today – he's taken it to his bed.' 'Ugh' said Tracy, 'Oh come on' said all the girls 'let's go…' and Janet led them down to an unused loose box where, for the moment, the kittens had a very snug bed.

'We want to see your Vietnamese pot-bellied pigs,' said Christopher, 'we've got pigs at the farm, but not pot-bellied, but I bet they st...nk, er, smell' He giggled at the thought. 'My Dad says all pigs st...nk, er, smell.'

'OK, let's go, but I have to tell you *my* pigs don't smell *they* are ladies.'

I invited the waiting gang of lads onto the small patch of grass, which led to the spare stable at the end of the barn where T and T, the two pigs, lived.

Apart from an enormous mound of clean straw and a heap of droppings in the corner of the stable, there was nothing to be seen, as we all hung over the stable-door entrance to the 'pig box'.

'Jason, our little pony, used to live here,' I commented 'but now he has his own place further up the field.

A deep guttural sound assaulted our ears.

Shh, shh,' I cautioned 'what can you hear?'

'Snoring?' said Patrick.

They all snorted in derision.

'No oo...' they choroused.

At that, the heap of straw got up and moved menacingly towards us. The boys took an involuntary step backwards.

The heap divided itself roughly in half, one still came towards us while the other half retreated to the corner and delicately performed its business of bowel evacuation, dropping bits of straw in the process.

The vision in front of us gave a great shake and revealed a large, black, bulbous body with a squashed looking face, tiny eyes almost hidden by folds of black skin and a mobile flat piggy nose sniffing eagerly at us.

All in all, it was not a pretty sight.

'Hallo, Tina 'I greeted her lovingly, 'are you hungry?' and at those magic words she squealed in pleasure, took another step forward and opened her mouth.

I handed a large apple to Patrick. 'Do you want to go in and give her that? She'll be your best friend?'

He looked appalled.

'What about you Chris, you're used to pigs. Give her the apple, she doesn't bite, she adores people who feed her.'

'My Dad says never give treats...' and he moved behind Patrick in case I pushed him in first.

'I'll go,' volunteered Robin, 'I've got some bread in my pocket, from my snack, I'll go in.' with that, he girded his loins, opened the door and slid into the loose box, holding the apple pig-mouth high. Tina opened her mouth a little wider and gently but *very* firmly took the whole apple between her teeth backing towards her pile of straw, sat down heavily, and started munching happily. The other heap, having shed her straw with a short sharp shake, moved smartly forward intent on getting her own apple as soon as possible, *if* we didn't mind.

Robin yelped, opened the door a crack and retreated smartly.

'Oh poor girl, here's yours Tutty,' and I went in, gave her the apple whilst scratching her neck in the process. She stopped in mid bite and leaned into my moving hand rubbing herself in ecstasy, apple still visible in the corner of her mouth.

'Don't worry boys, they are quite used to visitors, give them an apple, or a banana and a scratch, don't be scared. They don't bite, all they do is lean a bit. They will quite like you, as long as you don't interfere with their bed.' And I pointed to the heaped clean straw that occupied about half the floor space.

'You can all come in, bring an apple with you from the bucket in the corner of the barn, over there. Give them a scratch and talk to them – they will talk back. You won't understand of course, because they don't speak English they only speak Vietnamese!' The boys looked at me unbelievingly but ventured in one by one. Apple in one hand, the other ready to scratch. My brave boys from the Top Class soon surrounded T and T.

Once the pigs realised they had captive back scratchers and seemingly endless apples they were hooked.

They leaned, they chewed and finally they collapsed on to their luxury bed of straw, benign grins on their black piggy faces.

They were in Pig Heaven!

That is until David M decided to try a piggy sleep-over on their beloved straw.

As they heard the unusual rustling of their bed their ears pricked, their curly tails began to wag like angry cats. As one, they hauled themselves to their feet and began a high-pitched squeal in fluent Vietnamese.

Their eyesight was not too good, so it took a few seconds to locate the source of the rustle. Everyone put their hands over their ears and retreated from the vicinity in good order. Except David, who was pinned in a corner.

They advanced on him and stood there swearing like fishwives without pause for breath.

'Talk to them David,' I urged. 'Say something nice in a soothing voice, once they hear you trying to be friendly they will gradually stop the noise, and probably dig themselves in for the night. They must be tired.'

'I am not talking to *pigs!*' Shouted David scornfully above the din, which was rising in pitch and volume as T and T, felt more and more hard done by. 'What can I say anyway?'

'Try a song,' I suggested 'you know the one we had in music last week. 'Sleep my piggy one sleep, fo-ond vigil I ke-ep...' I paraphrased. That might do it.'

David sang in the local choir.

My hidden laughter at the expression of revulsion on David's face was threatening to show. I raised a cautionary hand at the giggling boys outside the box. Neither pig nor boy would appreciate the amusement. We all loved a joke, though – and this was fit to feature in the best Laurel and Hardy film you could imagine.

As the sounds of Schubert's lovely melody floated out over the pig's backs, there was an instant of quiet. The pigs had paused for breath at last and the novelty of song was having an effect. The squeals died away, David edged out of the corner. I took him by the hand and whispered

'Don't stop singing, I don't think they have heard this song before' and together we almost tiptoed out of the box.

I am not sure the pigs realised we had gone, but as David's voice faded to a soothing lullaby they turned back to the beautifully deep bed of golden straw and began to cuddle down in it, using their mouths to throw the stuff over each other until they were totally covered once again. The stable looked completely deserted, and soon snores reverberated from wall to wall as my pot-bellied pigs settled down for the night.

It was well past their bedtime, and time for us to be going.

The girls had congregated in the middle of the yard, wondering what on earth was causing the Vietnamese swearing.

Janet had a grin on her face.

'Did one of the boys stand on the pig's bed?' she asked.

David sheepishly admitted it.

'You know what the penalty is don't you?' She said.

David shook his head.

'Mrs A makes visitors, and their friends, who start her pigs squealing, come and muck them out. The pigs *really* yell then, I have to wear ear plugs.'

The boys turned to look at me in horror.

'It's a joke,' I said 'It is only a joke, we don't mean it do we Janet.'

'Oh yes, yes we do.' she insisted. 'Oh yes David, we do!' and handed him her mucking out fork and a pair of rubber gloves! 'You can start now...'

Only the happy looking group of girls laughed.

****

A poke is a mediaeval term for 'bag'. When meat was scarce, gullible people would buy a piglet tied up in a sack.

Not surprisingly the sack would wriggle a lot!

However, when they got their bag home and opened it they quite often found a substitute! Usually a cat.

The poor animal was then fed to the family with the idea 'any meat is good meat.'

Nowadays the term would simply mean you have bought something that you hadn't bargained for.

T and T certainly turned out to be much more than *we* bargained for...

For example, once every couple of weeks, Gordon, a gentle, soft-spoken man would come and take out all their straw and put in a clean bed.

They *hated* him with a deep, abiding loathing. They always retreated to the far corner of their capacious stable and screamed in their high-pitched Vietnamese all the way through the process.

They stamped their little feet and wagged their tails in fury. Apart from wearing earplugs, Gordon ignored them and got on with the job of removing the old straw, bringing in a bale of new and spreading it to a deep thick bed as he went.

He cleaned out the muck, dusted that corner with Izal powder, and left them to it.

As soon as they heard the bolt on the door, as it closed, they stopped the yelling, made a beeline for the bed, and collapsed on it, quite exhausted with all their hard work.

They did love *me* though, the bringer of food, water, apples, bananas, back scratchers and soothing voices.

They enjoyed a walk about the place, usually following me like a pair of oversized, droopy-bellied dogs. They adored a hosing down with a gentle water flow from the hosepipe.

Patrick-the-vet found out that it was necessary to give *me* the hypodermic to administer any injections, such as a mild sedative in order to trim their feet. He found not only did they raise a hell of a din but they decided manhandling in order to get the needle in was not to their taste. Being pinned to the wall was not to *his* taste either!

They lived to a ripe old age of nine years, when, due to travel restrictions caused by swine vesicular fever, combined with our necessary move out of the area, they had to be put down by our long-suffering vet.

They had led extended and I hope happy lives. In their original habitat they would have been caught, slaughtered cooked and eaten as suckling pigs, at approximately three to four weeks old.

I loved them dearly, and mourned their passing.

Communion Wine

'...A fiery blessing with contrasting hints of brimstone, damnation and eventual forgiveness that will bring you to your knees in thanksgiving. It reaches deep into the soul and refreshes the parts other religious tinctures cannot reach. Alleluia!'

From a Report in 'Guide to Good Communion Wine'

Ruth, Lady Craufurd, came storming into my classroom one day.
As the wife of our 'squire' Sir James Craufurd, she was held in some awe.

'Is Jonathan here?' she demanded in stentorian tones. 'I wish to speak to him about a *certain incident.*' She looked at me.
'Well?'
Everyone stopped what they were doing and gazed uneasily at Lady C as she stood there at the front of my class, looking round the room. I had noticed Jonathan very swiftly creep out of the door behind her tall figure, as soon as she began manoeuvring her way round the children's desks towards mine.
'*He* will know what I am talking about.' She asserted.
She suddenly spied Tobias, Jonathan's brother who was leaning back in his chair looking deceptively nonchalant.
'You must know where he is.' She addressed him accusingly.
Tobias said nothing. He looked at me appealingly.
'Oh, yes,' I thought 'something is definitely up.' Before he could answer, I intervened.
'We would all like to help you, Lady Ruth, but we are in the middle of some important projects. Jonathan is not here now, so I would be grateful if we could discuss this matter after school. I will be here until 5.30 at least...'
She gave me a withering look,

'I am having afternoon tea with Mr Sutton, the Vicar. I must talk with him about the content and suitability of his last sermon. I will not be available.

However I *will* endeavour to speak to Jonathan's mother about his *scandalous* behaviour.'

With that parting shot, she strode out leaving us all feeling slightly shell-shocked.

Most of the children of the village kept well out of Lady C's way, so it was Jonathan's bad luck that she had caught him out in some mysterious misdemeanour.

He must have been a little careless, which was not usually like him.

As she left he slunk back into his seat at the back of the class. He tried to be unobtrusive but failed as he knocked over his chair just as he was about to sit on it. He was pink cheeked and breathing quite heavily.

Everyone turned to look at him when they heard the clatter. I caught his eye.

'Jonathan, we need to speak. Stay behind after school, please. You too, Tobias!'

Of course, the children were all agog with curiosity. What had Jonathan been up to this time?

'No questions now though, please,' I insisted, 'we must finish our projects before we go home, so back to work everyone.' It was time to get on with our follow-up record of our nature expedition enjoyed earlier that day.

I did know all about Jonathan and Tobias's unauthorised leave of absence earlier on because they had been spotted when they tried to leave their designated group unnoticed.

'Where are you two off to?' called Sandra, one of my parent 'helpers of the day'.

'We're going to do some research on the wild flowers over in that corner of the churchyard.' explained blond, blue-eyed, innocent-faced Jonathan, pointing vaguely as he spoke.

'We need some specimens to study. I know Mrs A will be pleased with us.' added Tobias

Sandra didn't know the two boys as well as I did so she swallowed the explanation and allowed them into the graveyard and access to the fantastic blossoms of the rose bay willow herb flourishing in the corner nearest the little gate from the school playground into the churchyard.

'Don't you go out of sight you two. You have a watch don't you Tobias.' He nodded. 'Fine, you have twenty minutes then you must come back to my group.'

'O.K.' they chorused and raced unheedingly over several graves, directly to the said flowery corner.

Distracted by calls from Vicky and Elaine who needed help with their wild flower collection, Sandra lost sight of the two boys, who had seemingly disappeared behind the bulk of the church.

Twenty minutes later, she was on her way to consult with me when she spied Tobias rejoining her group. She rashly assumed Jonathan was following. Unfortunately she was wrong.

It was not until all the children were assembled at their desks ready to record their finds, that I realised we had a 'missing person'.

I was about to send someone to ask the Head to come and supervise the proceedings so I could go and search outside when I spied Jonathan at the back of the class.

He was notorious for his disappearing acts at crucial moments so I was not pleased with him.

However, as his 'crime' had occurred during school time, I would shield him from Lady Ruth's wrath – at least until I found out what it was all about.

He and his brother Tobias had only just arrived at the village school. The family had caused a scandal among the locals at the outset, as the children called their parents by their first names 'Carol' and 'Peter'.

The villagers raised their hands in horror.

'What *are* these incomers doing?' One mother came indignantly into my classroom,

'I do hope you will not be allowing them to call *you* Jean *or* Jeannette,' she said 'How would you maintain discipline if the children take such liberties?'

I considered saying 'I would have no objection to any of the children calling me by my first name, as long as it was respectful...' but rejected the idea.

I knew discipline would certainly not be a problem but I felt 'our' parents were not yet ready for such revolutionary practices.

As for me, I was looking forward to a breath of fresh air blowing through our little community and very ready to welcome an 'international' family who had lived in New York and Bonn before arriving in our somewhat parochial village.

 It appeared their mother was studying for her Ph.D and their father worked away a great deal of the time, so the two boys tended to roam the village, sometimes getting up to mischief.

They were a pair of engaging, imaginative scamps and I knew I would enjoy having them in my class. Stories about them climbing up into the little room in the Church above the porch (forbidden territory as it needed a ladder to get to it), scrumping apples, sitting in any car that had an easily opened door, and wandering at will into people's gardens were among the minor misdemeanours the pair had been involved in. Their ability to invent logical reasons for being where they shouldn't be, became legendary.

They were among the first tranche of newcomers' children, with ambitious, professional parents. At that time, they formed an isolated group of two. However, it wasn't long before Robert W, who was also new, gradually became more closely involved in their adventures.

It was quite early on, that I became aware Tobias, the younger of the two, was struggling a little both with his reading and with his handwriting. He held his pen at an odd angle and was quite slow at all his writing tasks. He had endured quite a bit of teasing, so I resolved to talk about left-handedness to the class.

'Look at me, everyone, tell me which hand I write with?' I raised both hands, shoulder high.

Everyone, except Tobias, pointed to my 'writing' hand.

'Show me the hand you write with.' Each child showed me the hand *they* held their pencil in. Four children, including Tobias, held up a different hand.

'Come here.' I said to the four, who accordingly trooped out a little self-consciously to the front of the class.

'There are five of us who write with their *left* hand,' I pointed out. 'The rest of you write with your right hand. That doesn't mean that is *correct* it just means you write with the hand opposite to the left. Do you know,' I continued, 'about ten people in every hundred are left handed, and some of them became very famous.

Lots of artists, including a man called Leonardo da Vinci used their left hand. He painted the ceiling of St. Peter's, the most important church in Rome. Many scientists, like Albert Einstein were left handed too, and,' I paused impressively, 'so is one of the very first men that landed on the moon only a couple of years ago named 'Buzz' Aldrin.'

I looked round the class, and noticed one or two of the children looked a bit embarrassed.

I smiled at the four standing beside me 'It is definitely all right to be left handed; we are among some of the most talented people on earth!'

Tobias suddenly grinned.

'Maybe I will grow up to be one of the cleverest people in England,' he said 'my Dad will be pleased.'

'Yes perhaps he will, but don't forget something else; to be loving and caring is just as good as being clever...it may even be better in the long run.'

Jonathan was much quieter than the more outgoing Tobias. He was a thoughtful lad, quick and intelligent, but quite reserved and self contained. He did his lessons competently, as asked but not giving very much. He wasn't terribly popular with the local boys, although many of the girls liked him!

He was leader of the duo, and was mostly responsible for the scrapes they found themselves in.

Going off on his own, without a word, was quite a worry for me, especially as farmland and woods surrounded us. He would have been difficult to find if he had lost his way...

As Jon was quite anxious to make a good impression on me, he usually took care not to get into my bad books. His current burning ambition was to drive my ancient highly prized Land Rover. As it wouldn't have surprised me at all if he took the matter into his own hands, I kept my keys well away from the classroom!

I was determined *I* would create the opportunity for *that* particular experience.

I addressed the pair of them as they stood in front of my desk after class, as instructed.

'Well what have you two to say for yourselves?'

'I got roses,' said Tobias and presented me with an extremely mutilated bunch of droopy *rosa* intended for his flower press and nature record.

'I was too busy, checking the church to find any specimens,' volunteered Jonathan seriously. 'and I thought I heard an intruder inside the vestry.'

I raised my eyebrows. 'The door is locked all day isn't it?' I said.

'The key was in the lock,' countered Jonathan, 'so of course I went in, I picked up the candlestick by the door in case he attacked me and I crept to the vestry where the noise was.'

I held my breath wondering what on earth was going to come next, wondering if poor old Mr. Sutton, the Vicar, who was quite deaf and would have heard nothing, was lying prostrate on the floor… A heavy brass candlestick would have been a formidable weapon.

'The cupboard door was open, and there was a *huge* bottle of wine on the table and that metal cup we drink out of when we are in church, was beside it. The bottle looked too full so…' here the narrative faltered.

'Yes Jon, yes do tell me more!'

'Well', he said defensively 'I was thirsty so I took a drink out of the bottle. I spilled a bit so I used that metal cup. My Dad says you must never leave wine without its lid as it goes off, so I drank a little bit more. I couldn't find the lid. No one was there to ask either.' he added speciously. 'How much was left in the bottle when you'd finished, Jon?'

'Erm… a bit.'

Tobias was looking at him, open mouthed with envy. This was all news to him.

'And where were you young man?' I asked, turning to him.

'I said we mustn't go in the church, I said we must go back to school. I went back to school with my roses, Mrs. A.' said Tobias virtuously and he waved the bedraggled bunch in front of me.

'Lucky for you, you were seen coming back to your group; you can go, but I want those flowers pressed and written about for homework tonight. That will be your punishment. You need to catch up with the rest of the class. I will see you tomorrow.'

Tobias reluctantly collected his school bag and left the classroom slowly.

He really wanted to stay to hear the rest of his brother's 'adventure'.

I turned to Jonathan. He was standing there regarding me with some apprehension.

'You must tell me what happened next you know, Lady Craufurd is after your blood! I am sure she and Mr Sutton will be very cross with you going into church at all and the vestry is a private room, you know that.'

'I know,' he said 'but what if there had been a burglar there? I know there wasn't but there could have been couldn't there? I could have hit him with my candlestick, couldn't I?' I shuddered at the thought. He continued.

'Well anyway, after I had had my drink I didn't feel very good so I hid in the cupboard with all those clothes, just for a minute… I think I fell asleep.'

'Jonathan those were the clean vestments Mrs Sutton washes and irons for the services.'

He frowned, not listening to me,

'I've got a headache. I don't feel very well.'

'I'm sorry about that but I still have to know what happened next.' I got slightly closer to him and sniffed. 'You know you smell of wine, don't you?' He raised his arm to his nose 'I did spill some; I suppose it went on me. Anyway I walked down the path to the Lytch-Gate, I couldn't open it, so I climbed up on the wall and walked along the top of it, I was going to jump down at the end, but Lady C came along in her car and shouted at me, I shouted back at her, she was horrible.' He finished in an injured voice 'she made me fall off the wall into the graveyard nettles. I got up and tried to run back to school but the ground was all wobbly… my legs didn't work properly either.'

I looked at him.

'You do know that wine is especially for Communion. A little is used each Sunday. That cup you used is a 'holy cup' it's called a chalice, all of those things belong to the church. It was probably Mr Sutton you heard, getting everything ready for a service.'

He looked very pleased with himself.

'Did I really use a holy cup? Wow. Wait 'til I tell Tobias, he will be sick he didn't come with me. I bet he would've drunk some wine, I bet Robert would've too, I bet…'

I stopped him in mid flow.

'Don't look so pleased with yourself, young man. You went into the Church, and into the Vestry without permission, you took so much wine it made you drunk, and somehow Lady Ruth got involved and found out what you were doing! And,' I paused for effect '…you did all this when you should have been working on your nature project! I should take you along to her for punishment.'
He had gone rather pale, as I had been talking.
 'I don't feel well,' he repeated I've got a headache…'
'Sit down here, I'll get you a drink of water, don't move.' When I came back with the water he was sitting with his head in his hands with his eyes closed.
I had no doubt he felt rather unwell, but I wasn't going to let him off too lightly.
'What did you do with the church key?' I demanded.
'It's here,' he said and handed over the large old key. 'I did lock the door.'
'You will have to write an apology for shouting at Lady Ruth,' I said. 'and a note to Mr. Sutton saying you're sorry you drank his wine. You are going to feel unwell for a while I expect, and you deserve it! I will ask one of the big girls to escort you along the road to your house. I will deal with Mr. Sutton and Lady Ruth. I am sure she will have spoken to your mother.' he began to look rather worried again.
'I want you to assure me you will NOT leave our premises in school time again without permission, and certainly not drink any alcohol during a school day.'
He looked a bit more cheerful and held out a small distinctly grubby hand,
'OK,' he said, 'OK.' We shook hands on what he obviously considered a deal.
    Mr Sutton greeted me with some relief as I walked up his garden path, opposite the church, with the large key in my hand.
 'I have had a visitation,' he shouted at me. (His hearing aid was turned off, yet again.) 'Her Ladyship was very annoyed. That naughty boy was running up and down the top of the dangerous church wall, waving his arms like a madman and singing loudly. She stopped her car and told him to get off the wall. He was very rude to her.'

'Where were you when all this happened? Were you in the vestry?'
I shouted back, conscious that probably half the village could hear
me.

'Yes, erm, I had stepped out to look at my flowers alongside the
fence, when I got back the wine had nearly gone. Lady Ruth came
in at that moment and accused me of drinking it. I had no idea what
had happened. She insisted it was me! She was not nice about me
using church property for my personal benefit.' He shouted
indignantly.

'Even when I assured her I wasn't...' he stopped and looked at me.
'Surely *you* don't think...'

'No, no, of course not. It was that boy she saw. He is very sorry
and will write her a note, and one for you too.'

A twinkle came into his eye,

'I should think so too. He drank quite a lot you know, it was good
quality wine, and quite strong. I expect he feels a little unwell.'

He shook his head

'Oh well, boys will be boys. I remember when I was in the choir as
a boy...'

He was off on one of his reminisces that went on rambling at such a
mega pitch it always gave me migraine.

I waved a good bye and left him shouting happily at his roses.

My next job was to face formidable Lady Ruth.

 I called in at her house on my way home.

Heather, their long-suffering housekeeper, opened the door to me.

'Please deliver a message to Lady Ruth, it's about...'

'I know,' replied Heather. 'all that wine, and that rude boy.'

'Yes, but he is writing her a letter of apology. He *did* think there was
an intruder, which is why he went in, in the first place, *and* he feels
very unwell. It will be some time before he tries wine again! As he
was officially in school, I have decided that is punishment enough. I
am sure his parents will agree. Perhaps I'd better suggest he sticks
to beer next time, don't you think!' I said with a grin.

She looked scandalised.

'Oh no,' she replied 'Vicar doesn't keep his beer *there,* he keeps it
in his shed at the end of the garden, but of course Lady Ruth doesn't
know about that. Nor his wife.' she added

I thought of poor Mr Sutton escaping to his garden shed in order to
have some peace and quiet, caught between his rather domineering

wife and autocratic Lady Craufurd, both of whom bullied him about his sermons. Who could blame him? I certainly didn't begrudge him his very venial vice.

'You won't tell that boy about it will you? Don't tell anyone. He'd never live it down would he?'

I considered the 'good' Christian members of his congregation, one and all notable gossips and not renowned for their tolerance and understanding.

No, he would certainly have a hard time.

'He probably wouldn't live it down,' I agreed with Heather. 'of course I won't tell anyone.'

Mr Sutton's small secret sin was safe with me, my lips were sealed. I thought of his bleak little garden shed and felt a stirring of pity for the pleasant inoffensive little man.

I never did tell anyone about his hide-out either.

Until now.

****

I enjoyed the company of all the children I ever taught. However, I felt I had a special understanding with Jonathan. He came regularly for a quiet chat as I worked at my desk after school. He shared his childish secrets about his life. He talked about some of his ambitions, one of which was to drive my Land Rover; he was very persistent about that!

He wanted to travel a lot, like his father. He thought he might be a teacher like his mother. I am not sure his parents ever knew about the confidences he placed in my care. When he grew up, he went to University eventually achieving his childhood ambition of becoming an excellent teacher.

I should know, he clarified some of the mysteries of the working of computers for me, even though that wasn't his specialist subject. His final job was in an International School the other side of the world, in Vietnam.

It all ended when a conference on education took him to Bali. He died there, blown up by the terrorist bomb that killed so many and shocked the world.

His body lies in Aldbury Churchyard, next to the little Victorian school and not far from the flowers the two boys went to pick that day so long ago.

His brother Tobias, learned to read and write of course.
He went to university, joined the army, got married and eventually became an MP.
It was he and his young sister who travelled to Bali after that desperate tragedy and brought their brother home.

The shock and manner of Jonathan's death bit deep into the hearts and lives of all who knew him. As his teacher, and I think his friend, I will never forget him.

Adventure Club
Or
Patrick the Joker

*'Riding is the art of keeping a horse between you
and the ground.'*

Anon.

I was teaching the top class of ten to eleven year olds.

Some of the children were sons and daughters of ambitious
professional parents who were setting their sights towards the local
public school down the road in Berkhamsted, and some were
children of people whose grandparents and great grandparents had
attended the school. Most of these families were keen for their
children to get on but had no real expectation that their child would
make 'O' or 'A' levels.
Some felt such heights were unimportant, anyway, in the general
scheme of *their* children's lives.
The rest were a mix of farmers' children or farm workers' sons and
daughters whose parents were hoping their children would take over
the farm, or work on the land, as their forefathers had done. Wide
variations in ability and parental expectations made them an
interesting and challenging group to teach.
Christopher M had come in to school that morning bursting to tell us
something.
'I can drive,' announced the ten year old, 'I drove Dad's tractor into
the yard. He said I was a great export.'
 'Expert,' I murmured *'expert* Chris.'

Christopher wasn't listening he was too busy explaining how the gears worked to his friend Andrew.

'Mrs A, would you take us flying?' said Robin unexpectedly.
He was supposed to be writing an 'interesting tale' of his choice and his thoughts had obviously wandered.

'My Dad flies to Saudi Arabia tomorrow. He's promised to bring back some frankincense for our play at Christmas. Wouldn't it be great if we could go somewhere like that?'

'I'm not flying,' said David scornfully, 'they'd never let you have a go *actually* doing it. Anyway, I want to ski.' He turned to me, as I eavesdropped on their conversation. 'You could take us, Mrs A, you must be able to ski.'

'Well, I can't really ski' I replied, 'I have never tried.' Visions of legendary handsome ski-instructors floated briefly through my mind 'You can ride, I've seen you.' Elaine came into the conversation, 'You could teach us to ride...'

The mixed response of 'riding's sissy, horses are sissy' that with a sidelong glance at me, and 'I can ski already' and 'I want to fly' mingled with 'No I want to drive your Landover or a tractor anyway...' gave me food for thought.

Victoria chimed in,

'I know you've got some lovely piggies at your yard, and my Mum said you have two rescued kittens, I love kittens could we come and see them.'

'I do have a bit of a menagerie,' I said thoughtfully, 'Perhaps we could have an expedition there? How many of you would like that?'
The boys pooh-poohed the idea saying

'Boring, boring, pigs are rubbish, and anyone can see kittens anytime...'

'Well' I said tactfully 'we would probably have small groups anyway, as not everyone will want to do everything.'

The idea that an after school Club would give opportunities and experiences to the whole class with some pretty sharp learning curves both for me and my energetic pupils seemed a good idea.
I looked round at the expectant faces and decided I would try it.

'None of the activities you want to do could be done in school time,' I said 'but if we had an Adventure Club after school... how many of you would come?'

I looked round the group enquiringly. 'It would mean a picnic snack and then you would stay with me until about 8 o'clock. What do you think? Would your parents allow you to join a club like that?'

'If I could fly, mine would let me.' said Robin confidently.

'If I could drive your Land Rover I could stay on after school.' said Jonathan, hopefully.

A chorus of assent assailed me from every side – apparently, everyone felt sure their parents would want them to take full advantage of some interesting, out of the ordinary opportunities.

I began to feel the stirring of real enthusiasm.

'Right, learning opportunities should never be missed. Should they?' I asked

'Noo…' was the excited reply.

The necessary letters went out to parents asking for comprehensive permission for us to explore adventure possibilities…

The speedy hundred per cent response encouraged Mr W.

He had expressed some concerns about picking up pieces of child from the end of a ski run and worries about dangerous animals like horses mutilating one of the children, and as for flying… he closed his eyes at the thought.

He was not the enterprising sort really. But as he said,

'The responsibility rests on your shoulders, Mrs A., on your shoulders. So all right I suppose, go ahead.'

I patted his arm, 'They'll be fine, honestly.' I reassured him.

Our First Forays

Patrick was the class joker. He was a tall enthusiastic lad, son of a fellow teacher, Mary G and her husband Tony who was an expert on all things to do with canals.

Our first foray into mild adventure was the 'Grand Union Canal Expedition.'

Patrick made it a memorable occasion by his own special version of a big joke.

Poised on tiptoe on the edge of the lock gates he had called out

'Mrs A, Mrs A, can you swim?' and had dramatically disappeared apparently into the murky waters of Bulbourne Lock six or seven feet below us.

I abandoned the rest of the class to the care of the bemused lock-keeper and rushed to his aid, thinking as I ran,

'Oh my God, no I can't swim… what on earth will I do…what can I tell his parents…Mr W…his sister…?'

I found him crouched out of sight, perilously perched on a lower ledge of the lock gate, with Jonathan and Robin laughing hilariously - *not* crying as I had previously thought.

Not even his big toe was touching water.

'Were you worried, Mrs A? That was a great joke wasn't it?' he cried as he untangled his legs and climbed back on to the bank.

'I can't swim you… you idiot,' I muttered through gritted teeth 'you might have fallen in or got caught in the gates as they opened and pulled down in that dirty, weedy water…' my imagination ran riot. He looked at my face and suddenly gave me a great hug.

'Sorry, sorry, didn't mean to scare you. I can't swim either.'

His irrepressible grin showed again, 'You really thought I had fallen in didn't you? You were *really* scared. I bet no-one else has done that.'

'No' I said, thankfully, 'no-one else has thought of that.'

All my class had wanted to join in with our Adventure Club, one way or another. They enthusiastically elected to stay behind after school, snack packs in hand, keen to go somewhere new and exciting.

Most of the girls wanted to visit our stables behind our house in Stocks Road.   As we made our way across the field path to our Yard, I thought about my first encounter with the animal that now dominated such a large part of my life.

I had fallen in love with the United Dairies pony when I was about five years old. He had pulled the cart delivering milk up and down the London streets, stopping at each house while the milkman sorted out rattling glass bottles of silver, gold, or red top milk. He rested outside our gate, which was on a steep hill. Mother made the milkman his cup of tea and Dobbin had a nosebag of sweet smelling oats.

'One day I will have a horse for my very own.' I vowed as I hugged his leg and smelled the heady perfume of horse, sweat, and linseed oil from his harness. And so I did.

Some thirty years later, I bought Jason, a little Welsh mountain pony gelding, when we moved into our first country home.

We had expanded since then, adding four purebred Arab mares and a stallion to our stable, as company for Jason.

Figaro, a big bay gelding, belonging to Janet was also with us.
She was the wonderful girl who looked after our 'rural enterprises' when my husband and I were at work.   Figaro and Jason were to be the introduction to the horse world for my eager group of schoolchildren, tramping through the fields that sunny early summer evening.

As we stood outside the horseboxes in our yard, we were surveyed by a variety of horse faces leaning over their doors to get a better look at us. Asif, my Arab stallion really enjoyed children. He always liked having his nose tickled and a scratch behind the ears.

Next along the line, Sanyeh, a scatty female was not so friendly. Basically, she regarded most of the human race as beneath her notice. They were sent by Allah to serve the world of equines. Her aristocratic nose disappeared into her hay net as soon as she saw us.

Samal, her daughter was the total opposite she loved everyone. Her favourite trick was to open the top bolt of her door, and walk out into the yard, whenever she felt like a chat with her companions. That kind of freedom was not encouraged. We *had* to be sure the bottom bolt was securely fastened!

Last, but certainly not least, a nose about the shoulder height of my group of eager girls, just managed to poke over the top of his stable door. This was Jason, our chosen ride for the evening.

Janet had got him ready and she led him, trotting eagerly out of his box, looking groomed, fat and friendly.

He showed his love of humankind, especially children, by standing stock still, allowing himself to be stroked, hugged, patted and even kissed, in the hope of being rewarded with a polo mint.

Elaine sighed in ecstasy,

'Oh Mrs A, I love him so much, he is so soft and gentle, I want to learn to ride.

'Pooh,' said Patrick 'I bet I could get on him and ride like a cowboy, it's easy.'

'Nah,' said Jonathan, 'who wants to ride a *horse*, I want to drive *that*,' and he pointed to my old blue Land Rover parked at the end of the drive.

'Ok Jon,' I responded 'I get the message; our next 'adventure' will be driving lessons, OK?' 'Hmm.' was all he said. He patently didn't believe me.

Jason had a saddle, bridle and leading rein on, all ready for his first passenger.
Janet offered to lead anyone who wanted a ride, starting with a gentle walk. We suggested round our small paddock to start with. Enthusiastic Elaine was helped to get on board. Janet showed her where to put her feet and how to hold the reins and off they went into our smallest field, followed by Vicky, Claire, and Tracy, who all wanted to have a go.

Jason had not always been such an amenable little chap. He was six months when we first got him. He had only just been castrated, so was still feeling all male.

'May I have a closer look at him?' my horse-ignorant husband had asked. Not that I was much better, but I wasn't sure I wanted the seller to know the extent of our lack of expertise.
He went into the loose box rather gingerly and bent down to look intently at Jason's undercarriage. His bent knees and hands on hips told its own story – not quite a horse expert.
With a distinct twinkle in her eye, the seller asked me

'Is he used to inspecting cars? Do you think he is looking for rust? Jason *has* been done you know.'

'Done? Done? What's 'done?' ' I didn't know. I decided to come clean.
'This is our first pony, we don't know anything. Would you give us some advice?'
So, this kind understanding expert gave us the benefit of her many years of breeding, rearing, breaking and selling ponies. She was honest and straightforward obviously thinking that unless we were totally crass Jason was a good one to start with. Of course, we bought him – he cost just £25.

With some horses you get the impression they are only complying with your wishes because *they* want to. So, when Jason had his first rider on his back he decided to walk like a gentleman for the first few paces and then…gallop like a Grand National winner racing round the paddock like a mad thing, leaping forward and throwing up his back legs in the nastiest of bucks as he did so. John, my ten year old son, who was riding him, was fearless, and loved it.

He was laughing and yelling 'Yahoo!' in the best cowboy bucking-bronco rodeo fashion you could imagine.

As Jason raced like wind past me, I could see the look of surprise on his face. He was hoping this rider would scream and fall off. Bad luck Jason. When he eventually got tired, and covered in sweat, he slowed down and stopped, sides heaving and head drooping.

'Daft lad,' said John lovingly, 'daft lad, I don't think you will try that again.'

'No,' thought Jason 'no, it's too much like hard work for nothing. I'll never do that again.'

Thankfully he never did.

The girls finished their session and as one they said,

'I want a Jason, I want to ride him every day, I want to learn now Mrs A. Now!'

'That is future music,' I replied, 'maybe one day.'

The boys were now ready for their horse experience.

Jason was being led about by Claire who was trying her hand at the leading rein, with the idea of giving Elaine another quick ride round the yard.

'As none of you have ridden before,' I addressed the boys, 'we will stick to walking and trotting on the leading rein. If any of you think you are born riders we will talk about proper lessons for another time, Ok everyone? Anyway, you will need some jodhpur boots and a hard hat that fits properly, it is only too easy to have a fall and hit your head. Safety always comes first.'

Patrick, David and Robin muttered to each other.

'Jason only comes up to Mrs A.'s waist,' I heard them say, 'Easy peasy, I'm going to *gallop*' boasted Patrick eyeing Jason up and down.

'I'm not scared, my Mum has promised me a pony if I like riding, you can all have a go on it.' he promised rashly.

Jason had stopped, refusing to budge until he had finished the stolen tasty morsel of grass he had found at the edge of the concrete path.

'How tall is Jason anyway?' asked Robin who liked precision in his life.

'Just about 12 hands,' I replied 'he is really for small children. (He had worn an old fashioned basket saddle in his time, and taken a two year old round the village. The baby loved it and kept crying

'Faster, faster!' to her poor mother who had to run to keep up with the pony's rather speedy trot!)

'You boys are not going to ride *him* though. Janet is going to take him out to graze. He eats at night and starves during the day because he gets so fat. That's dangerous for horses.'

Claire and Janet walked to the field gate, where Janet took Jason's tack off, hung it on the gate and led him out to grass.

'Come with me everyone,' I instructed 'this horse is rather bigger.' The whole group followed me to the other end of the yard.

I explained that there were sensible safety procedures to be learned before being introduced to Figaro

I finished by saying…'so no shouting all at once, and they do have quite large teeth,' I paused, all eyes were on me, 'they just might BITE!' and I lunged forward showing my teeth. The group scattered half laughing and half scared.

'No, really, it is possible. All our horses love and trust us, so they don't bite or kick.   But always take care when you are faced with the unknown.

I arranged the children in a wide semi circle, boys one side and girls the other as Janet and Figaro trotted smartly out of the yard towards us.

There was a general gasp.

Figaro was a 15 hand bay gelding beautifully looked after by Janet, his owner. His coat and tack gleamed with polish. His large intelligent eyes surveyed us as he came to a proud halt in the centre of our semi-circle.

After little Jason he appeared enormous.

The boys looked somewhat stunned.

'Are we going to have to ride *that*?' asked David in awe. Even Jonathan seemed impressed.

'No-one *has* to do anything,' I replied 'You may sit on his back, and get the feel of a larger horse. Or you can stroke and pat him, or, here Janet produced a soft brush, 'you can groom him. It's entirely up to you. But first of all come closer and say hallo, he likes people.'

Patrick and Robin approached together, Figaro immediately dropped his head to pocket level hoping for a mint or a few random pony cubes.

'His coat feels very soft and warm.' said Robin. The rest of the boys gathered round patting his neck, generally making the most of the slightly scary feeling of being so close to the biggest animal they had seen outside nearby Whipsnade Zoo.

Janet started telling them about Figaro.

'He is learning to jump at the moment.' she said. 'I am giving him lessons.' She looked at Vicky, 'I think he could jump over you if I asked him to…you must be about four feet high!' she smiled 'I won't though, we use proper jumps with poles across stands. Horses don't always like jumping but I'm lucky, Figaro loves it.'

'Can I have a jump? Asked the intrepid Patrick 'I know I could jump at least ten feet high…' he trailed off as Robin and David and Christopher snorted in unison.

'First you must learn to ride at walk, trot, canter and gallop,' replied Janet, 'for today it would be good if you learnt how to get on and ask Figaro to walk round the field.'

'Here you are' she said suddenly, and handed the lead rein to Robin. Figaro, looked at him out of the corner of his eye and started to walk back towards his stable.

'Hey' yelled Robin as he was inexorably dragged along the drive, 'Stop. Stop'

Figaro ignored him and carried on walking.

'Whoa,' called Janet, 'Stand, boy, Stand.' Figaro stood. Robin caught up with him, rather breathless.

'Good job you've got a long piece of rein,' I observed, 'one of the rules of horsemanship is you never let go your horse. Well done.' Janet got on to Figaro's back and walked into the paddock calling all the boys to follow to the gate.

The girls and I followed, and stood behind the others who had climbed up and were leaning over to watch the riding demonstration. Figaro gave a great display. He walked trotted, cantered and jumped over the jump Janet had put in the field ready to show us all what could be done.

Figaro loved an audience and he performed beautifully, finally coming to a perfect halt in front of the gate. Janet took her riding cap off and bowed. On command, Figaro extended one leg forward and bowed his head too. We all clapped.

The was a chorus of

'Wonderful, I want to do that, I want a horse like that and please, can I have a go?'

One at a time the boys went into the field, mounted, with help from Janet, and were allowed to walk and trot in a circle round her.

The only one who declined was Jonathan whose eyes were still on the Land Rover.   When everyone who wanted to ride had done so, Robin proudly began to lead Figaro out of the field towards his box – and his supper- this time with no difficulty at all.

'Will you all thank Janet and Figaro, please' I said 'if any of you ever own a horse you will get to know that the past hour was a great deal of hard work for her.'

Robin handed the lead rein to Patrick and went over to shake Janet's hand, much to her barely hidden amusement.

'Thank you very much,' he said gravely 'I was so scared and I'm not now. I don't suppose I will ever actually have one, but horses aren't just dumb animals are they?'

Everyone agreed and there was a mixed chorus of
'I can't wait to tell my mum, thanks, and next time can I have a go?'
This last was from the group of girls who looked with admiring envy at the boys who had done so well.

We turned to look at Patrick the joker, who was dancing up and down grimacing and yelling.

Figaro had also turned his head to look in surprise at this 'puppet on a string' performance going on at his right shoulder.

We all started to laugh; enjoying the joke, and then turned to the business of making sure we hadn't left anything behind.

The heat was going out of the day and it was time to go home.

Janet carried on loosening Figaro's girth, and was about to take the bridle off before putting a halter on ready to lead him back to his stable.

Patrick continued doing his act, dancing with great energy on the spot.

His face was still contorted and he was pretending to try to say something.

Laughingly I went over to him, saying
'Come on, joke's over Patrick, it's time to go.'

As I rounded the bulk of Figaro's rump I saw that Patrick was rooted to the ground.

Figaro's great ironclad hoof was firmly placed over Patrick's smaller plimsolled foot, pinning him to the spot but totally unaware of the impact he was having.

'Walk on,' I hastily commanded and Figaro obediently took a step forward.

At that, Patrick gave a great yell and gave a huge leap sideways as his trapped foot was released.

He stood stork-like on one leg as I rushed to support him.

'Oh you poor boy,' I sympathised, 'we thought you were putting on an act again, it must hurt a lot.'

'It does' he managed to gasp. 'It does.' I could see he was very near to tears.

'Could you hop to that tap over there, I will run lots of cold water over it, then I could see if you have done any damage.' I put my arm comfortingly over his shoulder, as he valiantly hopped to the tap and sat on an upturned bucket thoughtfully provided by David and Chris. The water ran clear and cold over his foot as we took off his shoe and sock. He began to feel much better pretty quickly.

Unbelievably there was no mark on the foot, not even the beginning of a bruise. He had got off very lightly thanks to the softness of the turf after the rain earlier on.

I felt his foot and flexed his toes. There was no damage there. His grin returned.

'I scared you then too, didn't I' he said happily, 'I didn't mean to this time. It really hurt you know.'

'I bet it did,' I replied 'but can I ask you to remember something Gordon the vet told me?'

By this time, the whole class had gathered round to see how Patrick was.

'Yes,' said Patrick, 'I'm listening.'

'He told me to remember this:

'Horses are dangerous at both ends and darned uncomfortable in the middle. Who'd have 'em'?'

'I would,' said indefatigable Patrick, 'I would. I want to gallop and learn to jump over Victoria.'

We all looked at each other and laughed, even Vicky.

'I bet you will, Patrick-me-boy,' I responded 'I bet you will.'

****

Patrick got his horse and went on to join the Pony Club. He was eventually chosen to become a member of the Polo Team, which was to play in a competition match at Cowdray Park where various illustrious members of the Royal family had played. A great honour! His mother and I accompanied him for this exciting event. Our duties included sleeping in an ancient horse-box, providing food, of course, looking after his horse, when he wasn't playing, and also to replace the divots on the field after each match.

(Divots are great clumps of turf displaced by the ironclad feet of the galloping ponies as they swerved and avoided each other in the heat of the game.)
We were assured by Patrick it was a real privilege to do this little job as it kept the lush green turf in good heart.

We were duly grateful.

Flying High on G and T.

'Those magnificent men in their flying machines,
They go up, tiddly, up, up
They go down, tiddly, down, down...

They can fly upside down with their feet in the air.
They don't think of danger. They really don't care.
Newton would think he had made a mistake
to see those young men and the chances they take.'

Those Magnificent Men in Their Flying Machines - lyrics 1969

'Our Dad has flown to Saudi Arabia – again.' announced Robin and Andrew H. '*we* want to fly on a jet plane, it's not fair!'
Their father worked for an oil company and frequently had exciting flights to foreign places sometimes bringing back wonders for us to look at. The most recent contribution to our class treasures was a quantity of small amber crystals filling a white cotton bag. Andrew presented these to me for use in our Christmas play. Everyone was amazed to be able to smell, hold and feel real frankincense.
'It's exactly the same as the three Kings would have given to the Baby when they visited him in Bethlehem.' I told the class. Our 'Mary' was unimpressed. She insisted on calling it 'Frank's' scents.' and questioned whether it was right for a baby - *her* mother wouldn't have touched it with a barge pole, she asserted. When questioned a little further she was very vague about the identity of this unknown, mysterious Frank. I sighed to myself and let it go, for the time being.

Folded neatly, under the bag with the frankincense, was a red and while check cotton square worn by the men in Saudi Arabia. 'It is called a '*Ghutra,*' Robin explained, 'my Dad says the men fold it in a triangle and wear it on their heads. A heavy piece of black cord keeps it on. I expect it would be like a sort of sun hat. My Dad says it gets really hot out there.' He paused, 'Anyway, never mind about that, I want to fly. My Dad flies *everywhere* and I want to have a go too.'

The enthusiastic chorus of assent, mainly from the boys, prompted me to make contact with the London Gliding Club as soon as possible. Our Adventure Club was ready for its next foray.

Nestled into a fold of the Chiltern Hills on the edge of Dunstable Downs the Club was ideally situated. Gliders could float out effortlessly into the sunset, over the Vale of Aylesbury, turn on a thermal sixpence and glide home to roost with the grace of a swooping swallow. If not a jumbo jet to Saudi, it would still be flying.

Easy, quiet, effort-free.

Or so I thought.

The Clubhouse was vintage 1930's architecture with curved iron framed windows, white painted walls and angular art deco furniture inside, with a long bar at one end. It was totally deserted. I went in to wait for someone to come to the bar where I could hear noises in the background.

Outside, parked on the smooth green hill, was what looked like a flock of about twenty slender black birds poised for flight in the evening sunshine. They were interspersed with smaller, chunkier aeroplanes. An occasional tractor loomed incongruously over their fragile grace.

I was glued to the window, waiting expectantly for one of these slender creatures to take off when a booming voice behind me said, 'And who let you in?' I turned in some embarrassment, mouth open about to apologise for just turning up. The words never came.

A vision stood before me. He was dressed in some sort of white overall streaked here and there with oil. He had beautifully polished shoes and the longest, hairiest handlebar moustache I had ever seen in my life. His voice was clipped and precise with wonderfully modulated vowels. I was mesmerised. He looked and sounded as if he had stepped out of the World War II film 'Dambusters', or escaped from the half remembered radio show about 'Flying Officer Kyte…' It could easily be him!

'Well, young lady, who let you in? Who are you? Who left the blasted door unlocked again?' He turned his head 'Jimmy, where are you? Come here at once, sir.'

I felt like standing to attention and addressing him in kind.

'Sorry sir. Just walked in sir. Permission to speak sir.'

I wasn't sure he would appreciate that kind of approach so I thought again. However, before I could utter a word Jimmy appeared behind the bar. He carried a large bottle of Bombay Sapphire Gin a small bottle of tonic water and a very large glass.

'Here sir. Ready sir.' He said, putting the tray down on the bar counter and marching smartly back into the nether regions where pots and pans could be heard rattling about.

'Handlebars' poured out an extremely generous measure of gin into the tumbler and topped it up with a splash of tonic and one ice cube from a container on the bar. He drank deeply making slight sucking noises as he savoured the flavour of the droplets suspended on the fuzz growing on his upper lip.

He leant nonchalantly against the bar, one ankle over the other and asked for the third time,

'Who let *you* in?   What do you want?'

By this time I was regretting being there. I should have phoned and made an appointment. Flying of any sort would be too difficult to arrange if I wasn't even allowed to open my mouth. In fact, I was beginning to think I would beat a strategic retreat and come again another day.

'Handlebars' turned his head again, and shouted, 'Jimmy! Here sir!' Feet could be heard quickly walking down the corridor and Jimmy appeared with another tumbler in his hand. With a wink at me, he put it on the counter, and retreated.

'Well done sir, well done.' said 'Handlebars', pulling the tumbler towards him. The Sapphire Gin miraculously filled the glass three quarters full, followed by an ice cube and splash of tonic. It was pushed towards me.

'Drink!' he commanded.

'Cheers.' Slight lip-smacking and small sucks could be heard as he almost drained his glass.

'Let's get down to business, I suppose you want a lesson, or do you already have a pilot's licence? No of course not, chit of a girl,' he muttered to himself. 'A lesson then.' He pulled a timetable towards him 'Yes can fit you in on Wednesday – tractor tow, half hour glide. 6.30. any later and we'll lose the light.' He looked me up and down. 'Bring a man with you, we can't spare any.' He took another drink. I still hadn't had a chance to utter a word.

'Drink up m'dear, drink up.' I took a gulp, larger than I intended, and choked. He refilled his now nearly empty tumbler, no tonic this time, just a minute piece of ice.

He gave me an unexpectedly sweet smile, picked up his glass and walked out before I realised what was happening. I stood rooted to the spot feeling non-plussed. Gathering my thoughts I called, 'Jimmy - here, sir.' 'Please.' I added in case he wasn't used to females summoning him in quite that way.

He came bustling in with a drying-up cloth in his hand.

'Hallo, miss, I'm Jimmy, I work here.' he said a little unnecessarily, 'Don't take no notice of him, or any of the others, they're all like that, them pilots, they lives in a world of their own.'

Me and Dave does the work around 'ere. 'E'll 'elp you.' 'Dave,' he called into the seemingly endless nether regions, 'come 'ere! There's a young miss as wants to speak ter you.'

By this time the effect of the gin was beginning to be noticeable. I wasn't used to spirits and my knees were definitely wobbly.

'Come and sit down by the window, take your time.' Dave spoke reassuringly, a clip board in his hand. 'Did you, in fact, want a gliding lesson?'

A somewhat jumbled account of our Adventure Club ambitions, Robin's flying father and half a dozen anxious-to-fly boys came tumbling out.

I finished the little saga with the words

'It would be heaven to float in the sky, such an experience.'

'Erm, it's not *quite* like that.' He said 'Have you ever flown?' I shook my head.

'Look out of the window now and you will see how we do things here.'

Peering through the glass, I saw one of the slender birds being attached to the back of a tractor. A long rope lay supine on the ground as a man ran to the tip of each wing. A slender figure climbed into the cockpit in front and the lid gently closed. The tractor began to chug forward down the slight slope. The rope tightened and the glider began to move slowly. The tractor gathered speed, followed by the glider whose wings were held level by the men on either side. Suddenly, it was caught by the air underneath and rose from the ground at an alarmingly steep angle, the tractor pulling it all the time. It seemed to take off, drop the rope and swoop up into the blue all in one swift movement. The great bear of the tractor still chugged down the hill with the men who had held the wings running fast in its wake.

'That's it.' said Dave grinning slightly at the look of horror on my face. 'It's very safe you know, we have only had one fatal accident in all the years we have been operating.

'I could *NOT* go up nose first like that' I blurted out desperately, 'there must be another way. Couldn't I have a real plane with an engine, instead?'

'We don't have a license to use our small planes for passengers,' he said 'only the gliders. Of course, you could bring your boys and not go up yourself...'

'Oh no, I replied, 'I couldn't, I'd never live it down.' My hand instinctively went for the G and T still reposing on the window ledge. Dutch courage might be a solution I thought hopefully. How much gin would it take after all...?

Although Dave was a little concerned at the age of the lads - they were all under eleven years old - he proved very helpful and co-operative. We finished our session with the arrangement that I would bring six keen boys, a couple of men and the necessary letters of permission from school and parents the following Wednesday evening at 6.30 pm, GMT. Sharp.

The leaflet he handed me gave instructions about suitable clothing and footwear.

We were ready for our first flight.

I was greeted with great excitement the following morning everyone clustered round anxious to hear the result of my visit.

'Are we going up in a jumbo jet?' asked David 'will it come and land in our farmer's field? I know it's a big plane but the field is'normous.'

He was laughed to scorn. 'We would need a really long runway,' said Jonathan, 'anyway it would cost too much for the diesel, wouldn't it Mrs A?'

'Good thought Jon,' I replied 'Actually we're going in my Land Rover to Dunstable Downs for our first attempt…we're not *really* going in a jet. They would never let you fly one without training. We will be using a plane without an engine at all.' I finished the sentence in a bit of a rush, anxious to break the news gently that we were not going to join the jet-set just yet.

Only Andrew looked as if he knew what I was talking about. The rest of the class looked disbelievingly at me.

'How can a plane fly with nothing to make it go?' asked Tobias. 'We aren't going up in a balloon, surely,' he added scornfully 'that's not real flying!'

'Oh no we'll save the balloon experience for another day' I said. 'Our visit to Dunstable Flying Club will be like a training session, just to get the feel of being in the air. If you really like it then we can talk about what you would have to do to fly a large plane with a powerful engine. You would have to get a pilot's licence – similar to a driving licence for a car.'

We spent the next days rifling though books about thermals, gliders, small planes, RAF fighters and helicopters. The local librarian entered into the spirit of the thing and found us a great deal to look at, inwardly digest and discuss.

We learnt a lot that week. We weather watched with an expert's eye, wind watched with an anemometer and did various experiments with paper planes over a fan heater to get some idea of how thermals worked. My class and I focussed on the TV weather forecast, most of them greeting me each morning with remarks like:

'Little wind today Mrs A' or 'too gusty for safety this morning *and* it looks like rain.' My children could be seen studying the sky intently, notebook in hand, ready to record the slightest change in the cloud patterns, or the laziest movement of the little black anemometer we had fixed outside our class room windows on a makeshift stand made from the bird table. Even the most timid in the class who decided flying was not for them enthusiastically reported on weather conditions. Some were heard advising on the warmest jumper suitable for cruising at a thousand feet, probably the highest we would venture.

As the fateful Wednesday drew near my sleep was more and more disturbed. I dreamt of losing a child or two out of the cockpit without a parachute. Or, worst of all, a gale suddenly blowing an engineless, rudderless plane away over Dunstable Downs filled with my six lads, never to be seen again.

I was beginning to realise this adventure was going to be very scary. I have an irrational fear of heights anyway, and the thought of a nose-up, speedy ascent, in a plane with no engine being pulled by an earthbound tractor left me weak at the knees and light in the head. I wondered how I could wriggle myself out of the whole project. Echoes of my headmaster's words

'On your head be it Mrs A, on your head…' reverberated in my ears. It was obvious that none of the boys who had elected to go felt like that. They were full of excited anticipation. Tobias led the group with careful estimates of how fast he would get up into the stratosphere and the speed at which he would descend. Robin and Andrew brought in a note from their father in far away Saudi sending us luck and wishing he could be with us.

David was convinced he would be flying to Scandinavia over the factory his Dad sometimes visited.

All had decided they would have a race to see who could fly the fastest.

'You'll join in won't you Mrs A, how far do you think we'll get before the other planes catch up with us?'

'I am not quite sure,' I feebly replied. 'I must warn you though I am sure you won't be allowed to race. And you will have to follow the safety rules that the pilot will tell you about. There will be a co-pilot with each of us so he can tell us what to do as we go along.'

'We won't need anyone,' chorused my intrepid lads, 'we'll learn it all before we go. We can't wait, can you?' they asked.

'Mmm, nooo…' I replied mendaciously, although I felt as if I could wait a hundred years. I was rather ashamed of being so scared. What kind of role model would I be if I did leave them to it?

English weather being what it is it was just possible I would get a reprieve anyway. It could rain, be too cloudy, too windy or even snow I thought hopefully.

When Wednesday dawned bright, fair and sunny with a very slight breeze, I was very disappointed. There would be lots of thermal lift, perfect weather for gliding.

As I checked we all had appropriate clothing, including soft gym shoes, my stomach started jumping like a bucking bronco. We got all of us 'pilots' into the Land Rover, husband driving, and made sure the cars carrying our supporters were in convoy behind. Most of the class, accompanied by quite a few parents chose to come to watch. Or pick up any pieces perhaps, I thought gloomily.

The man at the gate directed the spectators to the parking area and told them to stay in their cars. We were sent to the clubhouse, where Dave was waiting to brief us.

'Good evening boys are you looking forward to your first flight?' asked Dave, looking very official in a clean set of overalls and his usual clipboard.

'Yes,' they said

'Where's *my* plane' asked Robin and Jonathan looking across to the window.

'There' said Dave pointing out the nearest group of gliders. 'You can choose one.'

'I want the one with the propellers' said Tobias.

'Sorry,' said Dave 'those little tykes are to pull the gliders into the air, to start them off, so to speak. *You* are being towed up instead of being pulled along by a tractor. Mrs A felt it would be a better option.' He grinned at me. 'We don't have a licence to let you fly those anyway. The gliders are those aeroplanes with no engines.' he added. He looked enquiringly at me 'Didn't you brief them…?'

'Oh yes,' I said 'I explained everything – and showed pictures, don't you remember boys? I told you, you would be towed up until your glider found a thermal. Then you would fly on your own.'

One or two had gone a little pale. 'The gliders don't look very big.' muttered Andrew.

Dave seized the moment to suggest the boys went next door to meet their co-pilots, to check over the safety rules, and to put on a flying helmet.

'What shall I do?' I asked Dave.

'We'll take responsibility for your boys now, miss.' he said. 'But we will need you to balance the plane. Go over there to that glider. Tobias, who has asked to go first, will be out in a moment with Jim, his co-pilot.'

I walked over to the plane feeling uncertain about what I actually had to do. The plane looked remarkably fragile to my untutored eyes.

Tobias came out looking very cheerful.

'Thank you very much Mrs A.' he called as he climbed into the cockpit behind the pilot. 'Don't forget to let go!'

The little plane had hitched itself to the front of the glider and as it began to rev up, the man with the two flags called out to me, 'Grab the wing, don't let go 'til the glider leaves the ground…' and he backed away waving the flags about incomprehensibly.

'What - hey!' I shouted indignantly 'I can't possibly run with the glider, I can't go fast enough.' My words were lost as the engine of the towing plane caught and drowned out everything. A man who looked about seven feet tall who I betted could run a marathon was holding the other wing. He sported yet another moustache. As he turned his head and grinned mischievously at me, I was nearly sure I was the victim of a 'set up'.

As the glider picked up speed, I found myself running like mad, slightly downhill, trying to balance the glider as she bumped over the tussock-y turf. The momentum carried me forward like the wind and as I felt the glider leave *terra firma* I was sure my feet left the ground too. I hastily let go. I found I was running so fast I couldn't stop until the seven-foot man caught up with me and swung me round to face uphill.

He turned out to be only slightly taller than me, after all.

'What ho, that was wizard, wasn't it? I always enjoy that. Keeps me fit. I usually jog back up. Join me?' My heart was pounding so hard I had to sit down. He looked concerned. 'Tell you what, I'll escort you back to the clubhouse, you can wait in there until it's your turn.' I got to my feet. 'That's the ticket. The boys are all being catered for by their pilots, they're not allowed in the bar anyway. There are some biscuits and lemonade for them in one of the hangars. They'll be having a guided tour.'

I was fuming as I strode back up that hill, ignoring the attempt at conversation of 'Handlebars-Mark-Two'. I was about to have words with our Dave. I stopped at the top and looked back at where Tobias and the glider had left planet earth. I could see no sign of them. The sound of another small plane made me look up. There above my head was another one of my precious boys, and on the far side of the slope a third glider was being steadied as the tow-rope tightened, the engine revved and the tow plane prepared to taxi down and gently take off.

The evening sun was still shining as I stood looking at the view across the Vale of Aylesbury, which stretched between the three counties of Bucks, Beds and Herts. Nothing could be heard except the slight rush of the breeze, sleepy birds preparing to settle for the night and the distant throb of the plane preparing to release the glider ready to join its flock swooping their criss-cross way in the cerulean blue of the evening sky. The sixth was just about to join them. Everyone was airborne – except me!

Dave was nowhere to be seen as I opened the Clubhouse door. I gravitated to Jimmy behind the bar.

'Evenin' miss, so you come back, I wondered if we would see you again.' He smiled and handed me one of his jumbo tumblers.

'Going up tonight?' he asked. Out came the Bombay Sapphire and with dexterous sleight of hand the glass soon filled with gin topped up with a dash of tonic and a small ice cube.

I eyed it hesitantly. 'Go on Miss.' said Jimmy and added some substance that made it a really pretty pink. 'It'll do you the world of good!'

'Dutch courage, here I go.' I thought and this time took a cautious mouthful. I went to the window to watch what was happening to my intrepid crew and saw what turned out to be Tobias make a smooth landing just about where he had taken off. Two men ran to the cockpit as it opened and helped Tobias to climb out, obviously chattering nineteen-to-the-dozen to Jim who looked bemused and amused at the same time. He saw me at the window and gave me an extremely cocky wave as he walked off with his new hero into the next-door hangar.

I heaved a sigh of relief and took another sip of gin. Across the airfield I could see Robin taxi-ing to a halt and yet another was preparing to land, further up the hill. Three safely back. I took another mouthful of the pink coloured gin in my hand. I managed to swallow it easily without a vestige of a choke.

By this time, one or two of the pilots at the other end of the bar had noticed my presence and raised their glasses in salute. I responded, thinking, 'I could get used to this.' I took another sip.

'Handlebars-Mark-Two 'appeared in the doorway.

'We're ready for you.' he called 'My name is Dick, by the way. I am your instructor.' and he smiled.

This was it!

It was then I noticed to my surprise there wasn't much pink left in my glass. I placed it tenderly on the window ledge.

I smiled benignly at them all and walked to the door in an exceedingly straight line. 'See you later miss, I'll save it for you.' called Jimmy holding up the remains of the pink coloured gin. 'Good luck!' I gave him what I hoped was a graceful wave without turning my head.

I felt like a lamb being led to the slaughter as I donned my helmet and listened abstractedly to the safety guidelines Dick was pointing out to me. In the cockpit there was a slight confusion over who was sitting in the front (I wanted to, so I could tell Dick where to go). Then the question of who was teaching who, was agreed to Dick's satisfaction, (I felt I should be in charge, on the grounds that I had become an expert on thermals only yesterday.) Finally, we were ready to start. The signal was given, the man waved his random flags at us and we began to taxi behind the noisy little plane. Dick's voice in my ear told me where to put my feet, where to put my hands and which way to look. The last instruction was wasted: my eyes were closed tight shut.

We gathered speed and suddenly, smoothly we left the ground. Our little tug was doing a wonderful job. I felt I could go on forever. I could feel the slight sway of our glider as we banked, smoothly rising as we turned. The noise of the engine in the plane in front was rather like a motor boat, steady and reassuring. I opened my eyes to the wonder of flying. I was high in clear air, the vista of the Buckingamshire countryside under my feet and the steady voice of my co-pilot in my ear – it was simply wonderful. Then with no warning whatsoever our little tug was below me with the sound of his engine fading into the distance, I could just make out our umbilical cord trailing in his wake. We were about a thousand feet up with no engine, suspended in ether with no visible means of support. I let out a screech that must have nearly deafened Dick.

'I want to get out!' I yelled 'I want to get out!' and I tried to undo the safety harness that was clipped to a hook somewhere down at my side.

'Relax,' said the voice in my ear, 'take a deep breath, we are still rising, can't you feel it? In a moment we will bank and turn – in fact you can do it, I will tell you when.' I took the breath and held it. All I could hear was rushing wind mixed with blessed silence. Like a gliding bird. My hand did what the voice told it to and we turned slightly, one wing lower than the other, and I could see the miniature cattle in the field below. My other hand followed the next instruction and we turned gently in the other direction that wing lowered and I could see Dinky Toy cars driving along the bias binding road. It was amazing. I relaxed. I breathed. It was a great experience. I loved it all. We took advantage of another thermal lift and I found my hand and feet following the dual controls as we flew ever higher only to turn and gently float downwards again. Why had I waited so long before this fantastic experience? I had missed so much. I felt a rush of adrenalin and shouted,

'Faster, higher, faster.' I wanted to soar like an eagle and swoop like a hawk. As our little craft encountered quite a powerful thermal lift rising off the side of the hill it rose more suddenly than before and my stomach jumped.

'Steady,' said a laughing voice in my ear, 'it's time we were thinking of landing. We need to negotiate the air currents carefully, the wind is rising slightly.' We banked more sharply this time and it was obvious we were losing height in ever decreasing circles. I could make out the Clubhouse and its surrounding hangars. It seemed to be coming towards us quite fast.

'We'll make a perfect landing,' said my mentor, 'keep your hands and feet on the controls but don't try to move them, just follow me and you will feel what I do.' I did as I was told, conscious of mixed feelings of regret that the experience was ending, and fear that we would nose dive directly into the green turf . The earth accelerated its rush towards us and our nose lifted as we taxied uphill and came to a controlled halt – more or less where we had taken off. I realised then, that 'Handlebars-Mark Two' was an extremely experienced and skilled pilot. I loved him dearly - I loved them all. I was back in one piece. Two men opened the cockpit, unhooked me and handed me down to the grass as if I was the Queen herself. I floated on a cushion of air, feeling the wind in my face. It certainly had got up since we left. I felt fantastic.

I became aware of my group of six boys waiting at the entrance of the hangar, stars in their eyes. They rushed towards me with one accord.

I was assaulted by the sound of their voices.

'I flew the fastest' asserted Tobias 'Jim says I am the best novice he has ever taught…'his voice was lost in the babble of 'I flew the highest…' 'No I did…'I landed my kite *easily* Dave said so' said Robin 'Dad would love to come here.' 'Real pilots often call their planes 'kites.' I heard from several boys.

I turned to thank Dick and his colleagues, regarding us all with some amusement. Jimmy at the window, was waving the remains of my pink gin at me, wearing a beaming smile.

Dave was standing to one side.

'I hope you enjoyed our little initiation joke' he said. 'Every pilot has to go through an 'Initiation Ceremony'.' He held out his hand. 'Congratulations you passed! Many people let go of the wing long before takeoff. You didn't. Well done.' I grinned feebly at him, my protests dying on my lips.

I turned to my intrepid band.

'We'll meet tomorrow boys, go home and tell your parents all about it. I am so proud of you all. I do hope it was a real adventure.'

'Oh, yes,' they all breathed, 'it was awesome, awesome.'

Tobias's voice sounded clearly across the grass, as they turned to go home in the various cars waiting for them.

'I am going to be a pilot when I grow up.' he stated flatly.

'So am I,' I vowed, 'so am I.'

I turned in at the door of the Clubhouse to be greeted with smiles and 'Top ho m'dear'. Jolly good show.' My pale pink gin had somehow been filled to the top of the glass, with its one ice cube bobbing merrily round the rim. I sipped it thoughtfully, surrounded by goodwill. Somehow, I was a member of the Club – if only for the day.

I felt very brave. I raised my glass.

'Here's to Dutch Courage!' I toasted myself proudly, 'Here's to the next time.'

****

Tobias took his experience seriously and got his pilot's licence during his stint in the army with the Royal Greenjackets in Bosnia before taking up his real vocation as a Member of Parliament.

As for me, I kept my dream in my head until several years later when I learned to fly a small four seater plane with a flying club based in Prestwick Airport, Scotland.

If I had been rich enough, I might have been tempted to buy a 'kite' of my own.

The London Flying Club still operates at the foot of Dunstable Downs. Somewhere in its archives will be the details of the children of Aldbury School and its pink drink imbibing teacher who joined the club – for a day.

Its reputation for safety and excellence is unsullied.

The Playboy Next Door

'What I don't like about it is this,' said Rabbit...
"Here - we - are, 'said Rabbit, very slowly and carefully, 'all - of -
us, and then, suddenly, we wake up one morning, and what do we
find? We find a Strange Animal among us.'

Winnie the Pooh, A.A. Milne

'Miss Forbes-Dunlop has sold Stocks School at last!' announced the President of the W.I. at the first meeting of the New Year. 'An American gentleman has bought it. He is going to renovate it and will also start a small school. She paused. Of course, it's the end of an era. So sad to see Stocks change hands. I am sure we shall all miss the girls singing in church, but perhaps the new pupils will join us when they've settled in...'

The village was agog at the news. Apparently, the American was well known in London, was friends with famous people, and intended to entertain lavishly.
All grist to our village gossip mill.
'My Mum says he's very, very rich.' Philip told us during our daily news session, 'she is going to try for a job up there. Maybe my Dad will get a job there too.'
I heard a murmur of interest from various children whose parents had obviously speculated on the likelihood of lucrative employment at one of the more prestigious houses in the village.
'My Dad says he's got a pet monkey,' Philip said excitedly 'her name is Dulcie, I hope I get to see it.' He turned to me 'Do you think we could all go on a visit, it could be part of our Adventure Club couldn't it?'
'We'll see,' I replied, 'we'll see, for the moment it is work time so carry on writing. I will want those pieces in by the end of the lesson.'

I was particularly interested in what this man was like. Stocks House was our immediate neighbour. Admittedly, there were several acres of fields between us, but I loved our quiet isolation way out on the very edge of the village. I did not want rowdy parties spoiling it all, and I hoped that he would still keep cattle and horses next to our fields. Each morning I looked out of our bedroom window at the peaceful pastoral scene, I loved it.

Reports he had made his money in publishing, he ran a gambling den, he was a multi-millionaire flew round the village. Some of us wondered what a rich American would find to do in our quaint English, very conservative village.

Speculation was rife as soon as the renovation work began. How was he going to change the 'shabby chic' of the upper class girls' school into the opulent décor the villagers imagined a rich American would want? Stocks House was a Georgian gem, he would be restricted by the Listed Buildings rules so he couldn't do anything too drastic to the house itself - we hoped.

The most interesting piece of news to date was that the new owner had commissioned an extremely large and elaborate bed from a small local firm of furniture designers.

'My mum says it's the biggest bed she has ever seen, big enough for a least six people and it's going in the best bedroom at the front of the house,' said Tracy 'AND...' her voice dropped mysteriously as she whispered something to the two girls sitting either side of her.

'AND what?' said Robert scornfully 'AND what, you gotta tell us.'

'We-ell, e my mum says Victor's got *black* sheets. Shiny and brand new.' said Tracy a little defiantly. 'I don't know no more, but she said they was very slippy when she made the bed.'

The boys lost interest in the subject of sheets and went back to the experiment on magnets I had given them to do.

But Victoria chipped in with,

'I reckon they're *satin*, black *satin*, my mum was telling Auntie Beryl all about them.' Obviously, there was great interest in the black satin sheets among the local housewives. I did feel that black satin was a rather decadent touch. I preferred my pretty cotton duvet covers from John Lewis. However, that information paled into insignificance when we heard that a *Jacuzzi* was being installed in the room adjacent to the orangery. No one had ever heard of such a thing. Tracy, whose mother had been among the first to find employment at Stocks House was a mine of information.

'It's the biggest ever! It's like a sort of swimming pool, but a funny shape with warm water that bumps into you as you move round. It's got seats in it and it's the *first* in England. Victor loves his Jacuzzi he has parties in it.' She informed an entranced and incredulous audience.

'You must be making that up – no one could have a party in water which bumps into you.' asserted Stephen. 'You'd fall over all the time.'

'Well, Victor does, and he drinks champagne when he is in it.' responded Tracy firmly, 'and anyway he sits on the seats, so there! You can't fall over then, can you?' she took a deep breath, 'AND he has his own special lavatory paper!' They all turned to look at her.

'What kind of special,' asked Jon, 'is it gold plated?' Everyone laughed.

'It would feel very scratchy when you...' began Andrew.

'Enough!' I commanded 'I am tired of hearing about it all, there are more interesting things to discuss than Victor's lavatory paper. Let's think about our science project.' Everyone got out their project cards and began to work quietly hoping I would give them the promised afternoon exploratory walk in the woods hunting for local fungi.

'I'm sorry, Mrs A,' said Tracy quietly to me, 'but Victor really does have special soft cream lavatory paper with VL on it in a sort of brown colour, I've seen it. It matches the wooden lavatory seat.'

'*I'm* sorry Tracy, but please don't talk about Stocks anymore. We don't want lots of stories going about before he has even moved in do we, it's not very kind, is it?'

I had begun to think there was a surreal quality to the putative goings on at the-house-next-door. In spite of this, I resolved to welcome the man in our traditional village manner. Maybe with a pot of homemade jam and half a dozen of my best new laid eggs from my prized chickens.

I might invite him and his wife Marilyn for coffee I thought. It must be hard to move into a foreign country, with few friends.

The first indication that we were in for a shock-horror or two was when Chris came into class one day...

'There are going to be bunnies up at Stocks, they're arriving just after Victor. He's coming next week. The bunnies are going to school!' he announced. We all laughed.

'Bunnies! Bunnies! What *do* you mean,' asked Elaine, 'you sound like a real baby. Bunnies don't go to school, who told you that? Anyway don't you mean 'rabbits'?' Chris looked a bit embarrassed.

'Well, my Dad was telling my Mum, I sort of heard it when I was eating my breakfast. He said there was going to be a club for bunnies up at Stocks. Dad prob'ly forgot I was there.' he added.

'I think you probably misheard Chris,' I said firmly 'anyway no more Stocks talk in class, remember?'

Chris came from a prosperous farming family who lived in Stocks Farm House the other side of Stocks House, only a stone's throw up the road from me. I decided I would visit Geoff, father to Chris and Mia, both in my class. He was sure to know what was going on as he farmed the land surrounding Stocks House and would probably already have met the new owner.

He had. He was also a mine of startling information.

I met him at the entrance to his Yard as he was riding home from checking his cattle. He was on his bicycle, his two small Jack Russells perched cheekily in the basket on the front.

'Hallo there, Teacher, come to find out about our new neighbour?' he laughed. 'Your husband Graham might enjoy the news I've got.' He went on to tell me that our neighbour was Victor Lownes, partner to American Hugh Hefner of Playboy fame. He had been introduced to Miss Forbes-Dunlop somewhere in London and had persuaded her to sell what was then Stocks School - at an extremely good price, about £15,000!

'What might interest Graham particularly,' he paused dramatically, 'is that his partner, Marilyn Cole, recently featured as a centre fold model in Playboy magazine. With mostly no clothes on!'

I was not sure what that meant; *mostly*? I had never heard of the magazine anyway. I was more interested in the prospect of new teachers to talk to; teaching in a small village school slightly isolates one from the main teaching community

'But what's all this about starting a new school then?' I asked. 'Is that just village gossip?'

'Oh no,' said Geoff, 'that's true. He is starting a croupier school in Stocks Chapel, it's been deconsecrated and there's no room in the house anyway.' I felt slightly shocked somehow. Aldbury was in the diocese of St. Albans I wondered if Robert Runcie had conducted the deconsecration ceremony himself, as our Bishop.

My hopes on interchanging education ideas faded. I didn't think I would have too much in common with croupier teachers...

I then remembered the WI President's expectation that the girls might sing in the church choir, and gave a wry grin to myself, probably not very likely.

'Your Chris came in to class with some strange story about bunnies …'I faltered as Geoff started laughing.

'Didn't you know the girls at the Playboy club are called Bunny Girls, they wear a tail and rabbit style ears as part of their costume? They're famous!' I disregarded that piece of information.

'And is he a publisher,' I persisted, 'if so, what books does he publish?'

'You *are* a real baby, aren't you,' he replied 'surely you have heard of Playboy Magazine?' I shook my head.

'No.' I said.

'Well, he publishes that!' replied Geoff, grinning, 'I'll go and get a copy to show you. I bought it from Smiths yesterday.'

As I rode my bike slowly home, I began to realise that Victor Lownes was a very different sort of person from the people in my usual social circle. In fact, there was no one in the village remotely like him. The man ran a gambling club, published a magazine that featured naked ladies and had started a school for nightclub hostesses. I didn't think he would have much in common with our local inhabitants. Not only that, but he had the School Chapel deconsecrated for his Bunny girl Croupier School. I wondered what the Vicar and Ruth, Lady Craufurd, would make of that piece of news.

I continued musing on the possible views of our Aldbury worthies when the full impact of Victor's background came to the ears of our gossip fifth column. There would be some interesting reactions, no doubt about that! I suspected our quiet village life was about to change drastically.

A maverick helicopter was the first intimation of change. The boundary between our fields and Stocks land was edged with a row of mature poplar trees. One day, not long after Victor moved had in, we heard the strident sound of a helicopter, which seemed to be flying low over the field next to the house. I rushed to the window, concerned that our mare and her precious foal were not racing around, scared by the unusual sound. I was amazed to see it skimming the tops of the trees, sideways on, taking some small branches off as it went. As it reached the end of the row, it banked, turned and flew back slightly lower, slicing even more small branches as it flew. This was repeated several times. My heart was in my mouth as I realised it was getting lower and lower ever nearer to the ground. Surely it was going to crash? Tiring of the game it suddenly righted itself and flew towards Stocks House, where it disappeared among the trees and seemed to land there.

'Oh, that's Victor's helicopter.' Tracy said unconcernedly when I told the class about the amazing skill and foolhardiness of the helicopter pilot. He uses it to go to London. There is a place for it to come down in the field near the house. It was prob'ly a crazy friend of his, or his son, driving it, showing off. My Mum says men are all show-offs.'

'Flying not driving.' I corrected her absently. Victor Lownes obviously inhabited a very different world from the one I was familiar with.

Some of the boys were keen to know more about how to fly a helicopter.   'Can we have a go?' they choroused.

'Oh no, you must be content with your gliding adventure, you're all too young to pilot a helicopter!' I informed them, thankfully. I wasn't sure I could cope with a helicopter experience. All I hoped was that he wouldn't be coming and going in the wee small hours, if he was, I would need to pay him a protest visit.

'Victor's gone away for a week,' announced Vicky unexpectedly, 'Mum said he has told everyone that the neighbours can go and look round his house, if they want to.'

I wondered how many more parents had found employment at Stocks, it seemed to me half the village worked there now.

Sure enough, a day or so later, I received a phone call, asking me if I would like a wander round the house, at Victor's invitation. How odd, I thought, to invite guests and then be away.

My curiosity got the better of me though, so I went. The house had been built in 1773, and was a typical Georgian style country house. During its long life, it had been owned by Mrs Humphrey-Ward a Victorian author, aunt to Aldous and Julian Huxley who often stayed there. When I had last visited, it was slightly scruffy, bare floorboard everywhere and being run as a finishing school, by Headmistress, Miss Katherine Forbes-Dunlop.

It was anything but scruffy now, it positively gleamed with new paint. The front door was open so I ventured inside. Beautifully polished wood floors, flowers, antique furniture and pictures were everywhere. A truly gracious entrance hall. Through various open doors were glimpses of a grand piano in the music room, comfortable armchairs dotted round a large coffee table in another, expensive looking carpets, and gentle wall colours throughout. Whoever had designed the décor had excelled themselves.

I wandered into the orangery where I met a young, attractive woman. She greeted me warmly.

'So glad you could come,' she said 'Victor asked me to make you welcome. There are tea and scones, please help yourself.' As I thanked her, she referred to a list in her hand. 'Which neighbour are you?' she asked.

'Oh yes, you live next door.' She ticked my name. 'I know the Jacusi has caused some interest. Victor would like your thoughts on it, so come this way.' And she led me through the orangery, where a wonderful wisteria was in bloom against the wall, with the door into the jacusi room.

It did look like an extremely large bath, with geometric alcoves here and there, where you could sit, relax and enjoy the warm aromatic water, which was bubbling continuously. There were cushions and large towels neatly arranged round the edge of the room. Various potted trees were dotted about, adding to its charm. It looked a wonderful, relaxing place. 'It's fantastic,' I said to my guide, 'have you ever been in it?' 'Oh yes, every day when Victor is away. His guests can use it anytime, of course.

Would you like a tour of the bedrooms?' she asked. I hesitated. It seemed so intrusive to go round someone's house in their absence.

'You must see his bed, he is very pleased with it. It is an emperor sized bed.' I blinked.

'I have to say I have not heard of an 'emperor' size bed, but won't Victor mind you showing people his bedroom?'

'Oh, no, he is not shy.' She responded with a smile as she mounted the graceful staircase leading to the first floor. I meekly followed. She opened the door of the room at the top of the stairs. It was large, airy, and sweet smelling. There in front of us was the biggest bed I had ever seen. It was about six feet wide and probably six foot six long. It was covered with a sumptuous bedspread and topped by an ornate headboard.

'It is certainly impressive.' I said. I was thinking that he must have the notorious satin sheets specially made.

'Do come in.' she said 'Try it, it is very bouncy...' and she patted the surface. 'It was specially designed for him, you know.'

'No, thank you. I don't think so.' My imagination had started working overtime... 'I must go...er, I have horses to feed.' I said hastily. She followed me downstairs as I made my way to the front door.

'There is to be a special party, soon, do come we will send you an invitation.'

'Thank you,' I said, 'I will look forward to it.' Victor's parties were famous.

I made what I felt was my escape. I looked across the fields to our property as I strolled down the drive to Stocks Road. We only had a conventional, four bedroomed family house, with two children, a Labrador, Jack Russells and a cat called Parsley. In spite of the splendour of Stocks and its Jacusi, I wouldn't have changed my world for anything.

Victor turned out to be a typical overwhelmingly hospitable American. His invitation for American Independence day duly arrived.

We were all looking forward to Victor's Fourth of July Party. It would be our first glimpse of the rich and famous that Victor surrounded himself with on these occasions.

Most of my class were also in a state of extreme excitement. There was going to be the biggest firework display anyone had ever seen, and all sorts of attractions including a roller skating rink, which had been put up near the entrance to the swimming pool. Victor had invited his neighbours, and nearly all the village children to mingle with his usual group of friends and acquaintances.

Various names were being bandied about as being on the guest list. The most notable one was Tony Curtis who had recently starred in the film 'Some Like it Hot' with Marilyn Monroe. The whole village waited in anticipation.

Although the big day was only a week away, my thoughts were more focussed on what to do with my valuable Arab mares and foals during the undoubtedly noisy firework display planned for after the festivities. It was supposed to last a whole hour.

We had all begun to keep an eagle eye out for any handsome

stranger who might appear in the village shop hoping it might be Tony himself. We were very disappointed when he failed to show up though, especially when rumour had it that he had returned to America to start a new film.

Resigned to missing out on this particular celebrity, we relaxed and forgot about him. After all there would be someone else coming soon. Victor had a stream of interesting and famous people regularly staying at his newly acquired home along the road.

I had decided to ask another neighbour in the village to house my mare and foal during the Party night, for safety. On my way to inspect the suitability of his field, I paused at the end of the bridle path that ran alongside my house. As I was waiting to cross the road, Argos my yellow Labrador at my heels, I saw a very large chestnut horse being ridden extremely carelessly, and in my view somewhat dangerously, by a man coming down Stocks Road, on his way to the village. His feet were dangling out of the stirrups, the rein was very loose on the horse's neck and to make matters worse there was a lighted cigarette dangling from the side of his mouth. I put my hand up indicating he should STOP immediately. I was Chairman of the local Riding Club and took my responsibilities seriously. We were forever urging our members to ride with great care especially on the road, present a smart appearance and look in control. None of those criteria fitted this rider.

'Ho', I thought 'I am going to have to tell this character off for violating all our rules and lowering standards...' But as he obediently halted in front of me I suddenly realised not only did he look vaguely familiar but he was wearing a cowboy hat, a sartorial choice rarely seen on riders around our village. I was about to take him to task for his shoddy horsemanship and unsuitable attire, when he took off his hat and smiled at me.

'Hi there ma'm,' he said 'so you're Victor's neighbour.' he smiled lazily at me, replaced his hat and raised his hand in salute. 'See you at Stocks party. Nice dog you have there...nearly the same colour as your hair.' With that, he gently squeezed the horse with his heels urging him to move on, turned and gave me a warm glance from those bright blue eyes as he went. He smiled again, 'Hope to see you around, at Victor's.' His horse walked on, the man sat in the saddle as if he was born there, feet still dangling, cigarette still in his mouth.

As they both disappeared round the corner past the Recreation field, it took me another moment to register that he was, indeed unmistakeably, Tony Curtis! And he was just as tanned, handsome and charismatic as everyone imagined. My mouth was still open, words of reprimand hovering on the tip of my tongue, never to be uttered. I felt like a teenager again, filled with adulation, admiration and awe. I was really going meet him at a party…next week I could hardly believe it. I felt excitement growing. I shook myself,

'Grow up, you're as daft as the children in school.' I muttered 'He's only a film star!

By then village opinion was divided sharply. There were those who held that a decadent, reputedly loose-living promoter of gambling and goodness knows what else should be studiously avoided. Contact with such a person would certainly contaminate. And there were others, like me, who felt that prejudging anyone without due cause was unfair and unfriendly.

'Give the man a chance,' we said 'You can't believe all you read in the papers.'

Catherine, who ran the Over Sixties Club, extolled his virtues. 'He has been so kind to us, offering to hold a tea party at his house, providing transport there and back and has made a most generous donation to our funds, which will keep us going for several years. He can't be *all* bad surely.' The Parish council, almost to a man agreed with her. It appeared he was willing to fund several projects they had in mind to improve village facilities. Percy, Clerk to the Council, urged everyone to welcome the stranger in our midst who was turning out to be a local public benefactor.

'Victor Lownes' girlfriend, Marilyn Cole, has agreed to open our WI May Festival.' The President at our planning meeting dropped her bombshell.

'She is charming, simply charming.' She added a touch defensively. There was a stunned silence.

'What will Lady Ruth have to say to that, I wonder?' asked one member rather timorously.

'Our Festival is likely to be the best ever. She has agreed we can use her name in our publicity so we should have a very good attendance.' replied our indomitable President. Everyone digested the implications of her words, eventually murmuring agreement thinking of the almost certain boost in revenue. Lady Ruth's comments about 'tainted money' and 'profligate lifestyle' faded into insignificance.

Few had turned down the party invitation. There were hundreds of people walking up Stocks House drive going to enjoy Victor's Fourth of July Celebrations.

'Hallo Mrs A,' called Elaine and Vicky from just behind me, Clive and a few of his friends had arrived early and were already sampling some of the delights laid on for the younger guests. I was right, most of Aldbury School could be seen here and there, with parents in attendance – a real village affair. A courteous young man standing at the foot of the steps to the house directed us to the front door. Just inside Marilyn and Victor were welcoming their guests, who were milling around with drinks in their hands.

'Hallo, you must be Graham and Jean,' said Marilyn, you live just next door, don't you, we are really glad you could come.' She smiled a charming smile, 'Do go and get a drink, they are being served out on the terrace beside the swimming pool. I hope we'll have time to catch up later.' And she turned to greet a group of exceeding beautiful girls who had just arrived.

She looked great in a designer slinky dress, with impossible high-heeled shoes, her hair beautifully cut and her face subtly made up. I felt dowdy, dumpy and FAT.

'Wow,' breathed my husband under his breath. 'So that is what a Playboy centre-fold looks like in real life.' I pinched him, really hard. He turned to grin at me.

We wandered out to one of the tables by the swimming pool where we were offered a giant paper cup advertising coca-cola. It was full to the brim with a brownish liquid. It had four or five ice cubes dancing in it, I took a sip and thought what odd tasting coke. The barman stared at me.

'It's not coke, ma'm its Bourbon, regular whisky. It's real good for you. Sorry about the paper cup ma'm, but Marilyn was worried about glass breakages near the pool.' I stared down at what must have been a third of a pint of Bourbon and wondered what to do with it. I couldn't possibly drink it although my husband was valiantly downing some of his. One of the potted palms was just within reach. I hoped it liked almost pure alcohol!

We sat down under a parasol near the swimming pool on the terrace. There was a continuous coming and going of gorgeous girls and bronzed young men apparently sampling the jacuzi and then jumping into the swimming pool. It was very like a scene from a Hollywood movie. Marilyn sauntered by in a bikini.

'Hallo, Graham,' she said 'why aren't you sitting in our jacusi, it is very relaxing.' His mouth moved but no words came out. I was amused to see him blushing. She turned to me, 'If you want to borrow a swim suit there is a large selection in the changing room, do help yourself.' She gave us a dazzling smile, and moved on to talk to someone who looked remarkably like Roger Moore sitting at the table next to us. I heard his unmistakable voice responding to a remark of hers, it *was* him.

'I'm going to sample the famous jacusi,' I announced 'see you later.' and disappeared towards the changing rooms.

Picking up an enormous fluffy towel and wearing a glamorous swimsuit I found in the changing room I sat on an underwater seat in one of the alcoves, the water gently massaging the small of my back and bubbling deliciously all around me. I was alone except for a man and his two young children. The sounds of the party receded as the combined effects of the Bourbon and warm water had their way. I relaxed.

'Are you enjoying the bubbles?' a child's voice interrupted my dreams.

'Mmm, lovely' I murmured.

'Leave the lady alone darling,' said a familiar male voice. I opened my eyes and looked into the smiling slightly apologetic face of John Cleese who had brought his two children to sample the novelty of a bubbling bath.

'Sorry she disturbed you,' he said, 'we are just leaving.' And he lifted his little one on to the edge of the pool.

'Wait Daddy wait, I want to stay.' pleaded the child in the water.

'Time for tea,' he said 'Let's go.' He lifted his long legs onto the side of the bath and got out holding each child's hand as they wandered along to the Champagne and strawberry tea waiting for us. I followed his example, draping my luxurious fluffy towel around me as I went.

I decided to go through to the drawing room, and out through the French windows to have my strawberries and cream hoping for a glimpse of Tony Curtis. As I reached the drawing room door, I stopped in my tracks.

Jesus was walking in the opposite direction, towards me.

I did a double-take. Had I died or was I dreaming, or was this a vision as a reward for going to a convent school in my youth? I gave myself a thorough shaking.

'Jesus wouldn't come to a party like this,' I gasped to myself. 'I am seeing things – too much bourbon in the coca cola'.

I cautiously looked round. No one else was taking any notice of Him at all. We stopped, face to face.

'He's not very tall…' was my first thought and then I realised, as he smiled and murmured 'Hi...' at me it wasn't Jesus at all. It was Robert Powell. He'd *played* Jesus. In a film. It wasn't really Him. He politely stood aside to allow me to go through the door and he was gone.

My heart was thudding as I aimed towards the champagne and strawberries. I didn't think I could cope much longer with meeting all these celebrities at once it was just too stressful.

There were mounds of glowing scarlet fruit and multiple jugs of cream dotted about long tables, with assiduous waiters plying us with champagne to drink. I sank into a chair at empty table, glad to be alone for a moment, ready to enjoy the real treat of a 'Strawberry Tea.' It was only a few moments later when two men came to join me. They were amicably arguing over the merits of a work of art, and obviously waiting for their friends to join them. I tried my best dinner table gambit during a lull in their conversation.

'Hello, I live next door, are you a friend of Victor's?' I asked the man sitting next to me. He turned to look at me, a little too appraisingly for my liking. I could feel myself blushing slightly as \I pulled the towel slightly more securely across my front.

'More a business colleague,' He replied. 'and you?'

'I am just a neighbour, I teach in the village school, here. What do you do?'

'I'm in advertising,' he said and half stood, hand extended ready to shake mine. 'I'm Charles Saatchi, and this is my brother Maurice.' He paused.

'Oh, yes, advertising, erm, my name is Jeannette.' I shook his hand and carried on eating my delicious strawberries. He looked hard at me as if expecting some reaction.

'Have you ever heard of us?' he asked.

'No,' I said in surprise 'should I have done?' He gave me a

contemptuous look and turned his back on me as his friends joined him and his brother.

'Oh,' I thought 'I've been well and truly snubbed. Horrid man,' I thought of the argument with his brother Maurice about that 'work of art'. 'I bet he doesn't know anything about art, I bet he couldn't tell a Picasso from a – a - Holbein.' I consoled myself 'And what has art got to do with advertising, anyway?' I dismissed him from my mind as I got up in order to look for my errant husband.

I found him chatting to farmer Geoff, both lounging by the pool enjoying the spectacle of costumed bunny girls mingling with the guests.

'You haven't moved far,' I teased 'have you spent the whole afternoon here at the water's edge?'

'Oh yes.' they replied in unison, 'What better place can there be?

'It depends on your point of view,' I replied laughing. Bunny girls were only marginally interesting to me, but I sat down relaxed and happy to enjoy the beautiful people and the lovely setting sun.

As darkness fell, the swimming pool shimmered and glowed, illuminated by underwater lights. We seemed to be surrounded by fireflies as the side of the house, the potted trees and shrubs festooned with small 'fairy lights' sprang into life, Stocks was suddenly a magical place.

'How do you like it?' asked a deep American voice out of the shadows. 'I'm Victor, glad you made it, Tony mentioned he'd met you. He's gone to Hollywood. Flew today. New film.'

Our host was standing at the side of the pool, arms wrapped round two extremely beautiful girls. Each girl had a giant coca-cola printed cup in their hand and all three were taking sips in turn.

'The fireworks will begin soon' he said 'hope you enjoy them.' He detached one arm and waved at us as the trio moved away towards the house.

'Oh-oh.' muttered Geoff as he observed them, still standing near to the edge of the pool. 'I am not sure Marilyn will appreciate those three... Time to go, things are getting heavy around here.'

There seemed to be a general drifting towards the orangery, and the French windows leading to the dining room, where a sumptuous buffet was laid out. Not many people were sampling it though, and I became aware of lots of activity above my head on the first floor. Someone was beautifully playing soft music on the grand piano, I peeped in at the door. A small figure resembling Dudley Moore, surrounded by several females, was seated on the piano stool. A small audience sitting on the comfortable chairs softly whispering to each other completed the picture.

He turned his head as he realised I was there,

'Come in, do.' He mouthed. I waved my hand at him and shook my head. He nodded, smiled slightly, and went back to his music.

'Really time to go,' whispered Graham into my ear 'the fireworks will start soon, we had better make sure our animals are safe.' Sounds of the party were getting louder and slightly raucous, we beat a retreat down Stocks Drive taking a right hand short cut over the field and under a fence leading to our own land.

The magnificent fireworks did last an hour. The finest display I had ever seen.

I hated nearly every minute of them.

We stood in our stable yard, with me who loathed loud noises, cringing at every bang. I ended up hugging our stallion who also hated loud noises and jumped at every bang.

'We're a right pair,' I whispered in his ear. 'Nothing to be scared of old lad,' I reassured us both, it'll be over soon.'

The fireworks finished with a fabulous beautiful burst of gold, red, magenta and silver sparks lighting up the countryside around us.

This year's Fourth of July Celebrations were likely to continue well into the next day, but without me.

Actually, on reflection it seemed a little ironic we had been involved in an event rejoicing in the breakup of our Empire two hundred years ago. 'Nothing of importance happened today.' reputedly wrote King George in his 1776 diary on that Fourth of July. He couldn't have visualised the America that evolved into one of the leading countries of the world, nor could he have foreseen the bitter fighting in their bid for Independence.

As for me, I had had a surfeit of partying. I felt no desire to join the current 'AList' and no wish to be part of the jet set. It had all been an eye opening experience that left me feeling my original thought of welcoming Marilyn and Victor to our village with a pot of home-made jam and half a dozen eggs was ludicrous in the extreme. I wasn't even sure they would have appreciated an invitation to my house to sample Nescafe Gold blend and Hobnobs for their morning break!

****

The enormous impact Victor Lownes and his then girl friend Marilyn Cole made on our small village would pass into the annals of local history.

The various people who attended their parties ranged from the 'County Set' to successful business people and famous art collectors, such as the Saatchi brothers, Charles, who later married Nigella Lawson, and his brother Maurice.

Clients of the Playboy Club in London were frequent visitors at Stock House. They included many famous stars of the day.

Robert Runcie, later to become the Archbishop of Canterbury, was also quite a frequent visitor to the village. He endeared himself to me when he told me pigs were a passion of his and he kept some in his back garden near St. Albans Abbey. I don't know whether he really deconsecrated the Chapel at Stocks House or not, but I am quite sure he did not attend any of the parties there!

It was not until much later that we realised the significance of the background of the Playboy enterprises. There was no internet to give daily updates or gossip. We had no idea at the time of the notoriety of Mr. Hefner or Victor Lownes or of the various possibly dubious activities that were allegedly happening up at Stocks. To us Marilyn and Victor were simply generous, pleasant people, if out of place in our typical English Village.

I am sure some villagers, remember them as warm and hospitable neighbours.

I am equally sure others eschewed their company and regarded them as undesirable aliens, probably from another planet!

To me they were among the most stimulating, memorable and interesting neighbours I had ever met.

Anyone who has read Agatha Christie and enjoyed Miss Marple, will understand her contention that village life is a microcosm of human nature at its worst!

Certainly some of our Chiltern village people would experience life at its most dramatic from notorious parties, run away spouses, murder and kidnapping to mayhem and drama at the village fete.

'My' children of Aldbury School would grow up and leave me, some going on to fame and fortune and one to sudden death.

 I became part of that world and it became part of me and my enduring memories.